THE BREAD MACHINE COOKBOOK

Revised Edition

DONNA RATHMELL GERMAN

NITTY GRITTY COOKBOOKS
Lanham • New York • Boulder • Toronto • Plymouth, UK

A **nitty gritty**® cookbook

Printed in the United States of America.

ISBN 1-55867-296-6
ISBN 13 978-1-55867-296-3
Cover design: Frank J. Paredes
Cover photography: John A. Benson
Food styling: Randy Mon

CONTENTS

Many thanks to all of the bread testers and tasters who helped with these recipes. A special thanks to Laura Jane Wright for all of her input and help; and also to my husband, Lee, and daughters, Rachel and Katie, for all of their encouragement and help.

INTRODUCTION

Bread machines have made it incredibly easy to have homemade bread and its tantalizing aroma in our homes. I have been working with bread machines since 1989, shortly after they were introduced to the American and Canadian markets. When the first *The Bread Machine Cookbook* was published in 1991, there were no other books on the market, nor were there any manufacturer or company "help lines" available to people who had just purchased their bread machines. As a result, many people turned to me for answers to their questions on all aspects of bread machine baking. For five years, I published *The Bread Machine Newsletter* in which people from all over the world shared their questions, hints, observations and even recipes. Much of the information in the introductory chapter, in addition to the Hints and Troubleshooting chapter, is gleaned from this sharing. Please take the time to read the information as you may find your questions answered or helpful hints for your baking.

Even after almost 15 years, I am still asked three main questions: How did I test all the recipes? What did I do with the bread? What are my favorite recipes (in this book)? The recipes in all of my books have been extensively tested on all makes and models of machines. In fact, during the testing period for the books in the Bread Machine Cookbook series (over 5 million sold), my helpers and I loaded 45 machines three or four times a day. Machines were spread all over the house and the loading was done in such a way so that the machines would hit the "bake" cycle at different times to avoid electrical outages. Depending on where we were stationed with the navy at the time, the bread (after a sample was taken) was given to naval academy midshipmen, marine sentry guards, sailors on various navy ships, homeless shelters, the Ronald McDonald House and to friends and neighbors. It is really difficult to pick five or ten favorites from a book and each of my family members has a difference in opinion. Now that my daughters are teenagers (they were babies when I started writing these books), they eat whole-grain breads and don't freak out if "the bread looks brown"! When they were young, their favorites were Peanut Butter and Jelly Bread or Portuguese Sweet Bread (still is). My husband's favorites are English Muffin Bread, Peasant Bread, New York Rye and Dark Pumpernickel. My favorites are Portuguese Sweet Bread, Nine-Grain, Cracked Wheat, Multi-Grain, Irish Soda Bread and Oregano Bread.

The revisions to this book include new variations on old favorites, new recipes and additional information on how to use your bread machine and the bread to the fullest extent possible. If you are like some bread machine owners, you may use the machine frequently for a few months and then put it away or not use it, then take it out again. Or, you may only use it during fall or winter. The additional section "Getting the most from your machine," is designed to give you new ideas and make the machine work for you. After all, man does not live by bread alone....

I urge you to read the information in the chapters which precede the recipes themselves. Many of your questions will be answered before you begin baking bread, and many problems that you may have had will be avoided.

ABOUT BREAD MACHINES

It is important for you to become familiar with the owner's manual and/or the recipe book that came with your machine. There are a few pieces of information which you must determine about your particular machine in order to know how to make any recipe.

INGREDIENT ORDER

Manufacturers indicate the order in which the ingredients should be put into the pan. In 9 out of 10 machines, you start with the liquid; in the other 10%, you begin with yeast and then flour. For example, DAK, Welbilt and Citizen machines call for yeast and flour first, so the liquid will not leak through the hole in the bottom of the pan. For such machines, reverse the order of ingredients in my recipes, beginning with yeast. The really important point is that the liquid ingredients are kept away from the yeast until the machine starts.

RECIPE SIZE FOR YOUR MACHINE

You must determine the size of your machine. Machines are sold as 1 lb., 1½ lb. and 2 lb. machines. This may be somewhat confusing, because the weight of a loaf will vary depending on the ingredients used. If your machine manual does not specify the size of the machine given by weight of loaf, it is easily determined by looking at the amount of flour in the recipes that come with the machine.

In general, 1-lb. machines use 2 to 2¼ cups of bread flour or 2 to 2¾ total cups of combined flours such as bread flour, whole wheat, rye, oats, corn, etc. For whole grain flours, 2½ to 3 cups may be used. If you have a 1-lb. machine, you will be using the Small recipe, depending on the ingredients and flour equivalents.

A 1½-lb. machine uses 3 cups of bread flour or 3½ to 4 total cups of combined flours such as bread flour, whole wheat, rye, oats, corn, etc. Up to 5 cups of whole grain flours may be used in most 1½-lb. machines without fear of overflows. Most 1½-lb. machines will take the Medium recipe, depending on the ingredients and flour equivalents.

A full 2-lb. machine can use up to 4 cups of bread flour, although I find that 3½ cups usually results in a nice loaf of bread at or just over the lip of the pan. A total of 4 to 5 cups of combination flours (bread with whole wheat, oats, rye, corn, etc.) may easily be used and up to 6 cups of whole-grain flours. Some machines are being introduced as 2-lb. machines, but the size of the pan is the same as the 1½-lb. pan, and therefore must use Medium size recipes. It is necessary to keep an eye on the dough to prevent overflows. A full 2-lb. machine will use the Large recipe.

After years of working with all machine makes and models, I can assure you that there are some variables and individual preferences in the sizes of recipes used. For example, one friend with a 1-lb. machine (2 cups of flour, generally) makes Medium recipes, which would seem too large for her machine. My father, however, has a large machine and consistently uses recipes with just 2 cups of flour; in the identical machine I use 3½ cups of flour.

Unlike any other bread machine cookbook on the market, I give you three different sizes for each recipe. If a recipe is too large, next time use a smaller size. Most machines can make a smaller size recipe.

A few words about pushing the maximum flour capacity of your bread machine:

If at any time it sounds like the machine is struggling with a large amount of flour, add a tablespoon or two of water (or more if necessary) to soften the dough. If the machine is struggling, it could cause damage to the motor.

The sides of the machine may require scraping to help get all ingredients to the kneading paddle. Once the dough has formed a ball it will do just fine and may be left. If it has taken the machine a long time to knead the ingredients into a ball, you can stop the machine and start it over from the beginning, giving the dough a little longer knead.

One of the main concerns about using too much flour is overflowing the sides of the pan. Usually you will end up with a mushroom — the dough may cook onto the lid of the pan or may not cook properly at the top. The real mess, however, is when the dough spills down the sides of the pan into the inside of the machine and onto the heating elements. Cleanup is a messy, time-consuming chore (I've done it often in testing). It is difficult to remove all dough from the heating elements, but it burns off the next time the machine is used.

It is wise to check the dough during the second rise. If it looks too high, use a bamboo skewer and pierce deep into the dough to deflate it. Do not use metal objects which could scratch the pan. If you have absolutely used the wrong size recipe and it is starting to overflow, remove a portion of the dough. This enables you to at least salvage something!

BREAD MACHINE FEATURES

CYCLES

Initially, all recipes were tested using only the basic white cycles. Later testing has indicated that the DAK and Welbilt ABM 100 machines perform more consistently on the sweet cycle.

The same cycle may have many names. A sweet cycle may be called sweet, mix or fruit and nut. Most machines now have whole wheat cycles, but any machine can make whole wheat bread on the regular (basic, white) cycle.

You may have a specific cycle with a "beep" for adding raisins, a beep on all cycles or no beep at all. In any case, add ingredients at the beginning of the second kneading, or during the rest between kneadings. If you have only one kneading, add extra ingredients as soon as dough has formed a ball, about 5 to 10 minutes into the kneading.

Basic white bread cycles may have one or two main kneadings depending on the machine. Some machines have only a basic cycle which is used for all breads.

Sweet cycles should be used with recipes containing 2 tbs. or more sugar and/or fat (butter, margarine or oil). These cycles may have a longer rising time. The baking temperature is lower than the basic cycles for the higher sugar content of the breads.

French bread cycles may or may not have a longer rising time but all have a higher baking temperature to crisp the crust.

Raisin cycles have a beep to indicate when to add raisins, nuts or other similar ingredients. Generally the beep is about 5 minutes before the end of the kneading. The cycles may have a lower baking temperature (like the sweet cycle).

Whole grain cycles generally have longer kneadings and longer risings.

Dough cycles include the initial kneading of the dough and one rise, after which time the dough is removed from the machine, shaped, allowed to rise and baked in a conventional oven. This is the cycle used for bagels, rolls, pizza crust, etc. For best results, DAK, Welbilt ABM 100 and Citizen machines should be stopped after the first rise and before the second kneading.

OTHER FEATURES

As digital technology becomes more sophisticated and less expensive, timers and digital controls become ever more amazing and versatile. At a minimum, timers enable the user to place ingredients in the machine and to tell it when to have the bread ready. Some machines even have a dough cycle timer that is great for things like pizza or breakfast dough. Recipes containing ingredients that could spoil if unrefrigerated (eggs, milk, cheese, etc.) should not be used with the timer. As a general rule, only use a timer on recipes that you have previously made and with which you are comfortable.

Preheating periods are found on some machines. Basically the machine heats all ingredients to the proper temperature prior to starting the kneading period.

Crust controls are usually buttons pushed when you start your machine, such as basic white, light setting. Some machines such as the DAK/Welbilt 100 machines have a control knob. The controls shorten or lengthen the baking time by about 5 minutes.

Power outage protection prevents a short (usually 10 minutes or less) loss of electricity from stopping the entire machine process. If this is not included with your machine and you have a loss of electricity, simply remove the dough and finish baking the bread conventionally.

Viewing windows are a nice feature if you like to frequently check the process of your bread. It is always a good idea to check the dough about 5 minutes into the initial kneading to make sure that all is going well. If you don't have a viewing window, simply open the lid long enough to check the dough. Don't leave the machine open for long periods of time.

BREAD INGREDIENTS

YEAST

A living plant, yeast eats sugar and produces carbon dioxide which, in turn, mixes with gluten in flour to make the dough rise. Simply stated, without yeast your bread will be a flat, unleavened bread. Both active dry and fast-acting yeasts may be purchased either in envelopes (1 envelope equals approximately 2¼ tsp.) or in bulk. It is much cheaper to buy yeast in bulk in a jar or vacuum packed.

In recent yeast testing, the fast-acting yeast (sometimes called rapid or quick) consistently resulted in loaves that rose higher than those made with the regular dry active yeast.

Yeast responds to ambient temperatures. It may be necessary to increase yeast in colder weather or to decrease it in very hot temperatures. Too much yeast may cause air pockets or air bubbles. Compressed (cake) yeast is not recommended for use in bread machines.

LIQUIDS

Liquid ingredients should be warmed to lukewarm for best performance. The liquid should be warm or comfortable to the inside of your wrist — baby bottle temperature or about 110°.

Some ingredients which are used for liquid (fruits, cottage cheese) initially may be difficult to knead into the dough. It is helpful to take a rubber spatula and scrape down the sides of the pan and push the ingredients toward the kneading paddle. Once the paddle has picked up all ingredients, let it knead by itself for about 5 minutes and then check the dough consistency again for a smooth dough ball. If the process has taken quite a long time, you may wish to turn off the machine and start it again. This gives the dough with the correct consistency a longer kneading. Because the moisture must be pulled out of fruits (banana) or vegetables (potato or spinach) it may require a longer period of kneading before a judgment can be made as to whether to add more liquid. If lumps of the fruit, cheese or vegetable are still visible, chances are that you should let it knead longer before you add water. If you add water too early, you may end up with dough that is too moist. Should this happen, then you need to add flour, a tablespoon at a time, until a smooth ball of dough is obtained. Always use very ripe bananas for the best moisture content.

FATS

In bread baking, fats provide flavor, make the bread moist and give it a soft crumb. Fats used interchangeably include margarine, butter, vegetable oil of any kind, shortening or lard. Some recipes specify olive oil as it imparts a distinctive taste; however, you may use any vegetable oil. Unlike conventional bread baking, butter or margarine need not be melted to be placed in the machine. Applesauce or apple and orange juice concentrates (the frozen type found in the grocery store) may be substituted tablespoon for tablespoon. If using the fruit juice concentrate, try keeping a small can in the refrigerator, thawed. Allow it to come to room temperature or add to the liquid before you warm it.

SUGAR

A necessity in yeast bread baking, sugar feeds the yeast, enabling it to rise. In addition, it assists in the browning of the crust. Sugar substitutes for bread baking purposes include white or brown sugar, barley malt syrup, honey, molasses, maple syrup, and even jam, jellies or marmalades. Sugar substitutes used for diet purposes, such as NutraSweet®, etc. should not be used since they break down during the heating process. Honey is also a natural preservative for your breads.

SALT

A growth-inhibitor of the yeast, salt provides a counterbalance for the sugar. It also brings out the flavor of the bread. If breads are not rising, the amount of salt may be cut.

EGGS

A nonessential ingredient, eggs are sometimes used in bread baking to add richness, color and flavor. Egg substitutes were used for testing with fractions of eggs. If you prefer not to use the fractions of egg or to round the fractions, you may adjust the consistency of the dough with milk or water or flour as needed. One yolk or white may easily be used for a half egg. One large egg equals approximately 1/4 cup of liquid. Egg substitutes are based on this amount also. One half an egg equals approximately 1/8 cup or 2 tablespoons of liquid.

FLOUR

There are many different kinds of flours, grains or cereals which may be used for structure in your bread baking. As a general rule, white or bread flour should be at least 50 percent of the flour or grain used. A higher percentage of whole-grain flour (like whole wheat) will result in a low, heavy, dense bread. With the "rule" in mind, flours may be substituted cup for cup with other flours, grains or cereals. A detailed description of various grains and flours follows.

Prior to explaining the various flours and flour substitutes, some background information may be helpful. Any grain which has not yet had the hull, or outer lining, removed is called a groat. You will usually hear oats and buckwheat referred to in this way. Once the hulls are removed, the remaining kernel contains the bran, germ and endosperm. The bran and germ of any grain contain the majority of the nutrients. Up to 80 percent of the vitamins and minerals are lost by the grinding and refining of the grain into white flour (which consists of pure endosperm). A general rule of thumb is that the darker the flour (whether it is wheat, rye, rice, etc.), the more of the germ and bran are included and, hence, the more nutritional the bread. Any flour containing the germ and/or bran should be refrigerated for maximum freshness; at the very least, these flours should be stored in a dark, cool place.

While making yeast breads, you normally use a wheat flour base which, when kneaded, develops gluten. The gluten forms an elastic substance which traps carbon dioxide released from the yeast. This is the key ingredient in the wheat which makes the dough rise. Other flours with less gluten must be mixed with wheat flour to a maximum ratio of 1 to 1. The higher the non- or low-gluten flour amount, the smaller and denser in texture your bread will be.

WHEAT

The most common flour for bread baking is that obtained from wheat. There are several different kinds of wheat flours. Differences are due to where the wheat is grown (making it hard or soft), what section of the wheat kernel is used, or how the flour is milled and what treatments are provided after the milling.

All-Purpose Flour: A blend of hard and soft wheats that may be used for a variety of baking needs including breads and cakes. All-purpose loses many of its natural vitamins and nutrients during the milling process. Hence, it is usually "enriched" by replacing four of those nutrients: iron, thiamine, riboflavin and niacin. Bleached all-purpose flour is chemically whitened; unbleached flour is allowed to whiten naturally.

Bread Flour: The recommended flour for most of the recipes in this book. Bread flour is derived from hard wheat, meaning it is higher both in protein and gluten. You will find that bread flour will give you a finer grain bread. You may also hear this bread referred to as bromated, which is a dough conditioner used to enhance the gluten's development. If your grocery store does not carry bread flour, do not hesitate to ask the management to add it to their inventory. Bread flour is made by both Pillsbury and Gold Medal as well as many smaller mills, some of which sell via catalogs.

Whole Wheat Flour: Milled from the entire wheat kernel, it is light brown in color and contains all the natural nutrients. A healthy addition to bread, it is lower in gluten than the white flours and should not exceed 50 percent of the flour ingredients. You may also see this referred to as graham flour and sold in health food stores. Some mills label their graham flour differently than their whole wheat, as the graham contains 100 percent of the kernel and may be more coarsely milled, while the whole wheat may have had some minor cleaning and sifting. Every mill is different in its labeling, hence for our purposes, I call both whole wheat.

Gluten Flour/Gluten: The gluten protein is removed from wheat flour by rinsing off the starch. This is then dried and ground to be added to regular white flour. Pure gluten is slightly gray in color but does not affect the color of your bread. It may be purchased through a well-stocked health food store or by mail order. This is added in small amounts to your dry ingredients in low-gluten bread dough for a lighter texture.

Wheat Germ: One of the best parts of the wheat kernel, the germ is the embryo of the wheat berry. A wonderful source of protein, fat, vitamins and minerals, wheat germ can be added to all baked goods by placing 1 tablespoon in the bottom of your measuring cup prior to filling it with flour. It gives breads a slightly nutty flavor. Opened jars of wheat germ must be refrigerated.

Wheat Berry: Very high in protein and low in calories, this is the original form of the wheat grain before any grinding or milling. Berries must be soaked, preferably overnight, prior to use. They are the most common sprouted berry used for "sprout" bread. Berries may be bought in health food stores or ordered by mail. Store in a dry, cool place.

Cracked Wheat: Crushed, toasted wheat berries. Cracked wheat must be soaked a minimum of 1 hour prior to kneading. I always soak the cracked wheat right in the liquid called for in the recipe.

Wheat Bulgur: Parboiled, crushed and toasted wheat berries — sometimes used interchangeably with cracked wheat, but does not need to be soaked.

Rolled Wheat Flakes: Similar to rolled oats, wheat flakes are available as a cereal at health food stores. They add a unique flavor and texture to bread.

BARLEY

Barley: Barley flour will generally be found in health food stores. It has a very low gluten content and must be used in conjunction with a high gluten flour. Barley has a mild nutty flavor. Generally, barley flour is a low percentage of all flour used in bread recipes.

Barley Malt: A heavy syrup used in both bread baking and beer making, barley malt gives bread a rich, grainy flavor. Pure barley malt tastes similar to blackstrap molasses and the two may be used interchangeably. It is wonderful when used with seeds such as caraway, anise or fennel. The malt itself is made by soaking the whole barley grains, sprouting them, drying and grinding them. Available in a health food or beer-making store.

CORN

Cornmeal: Ground from corn kernels, cornmeal is found in any grocery store. Most commonly used is the yellow variety, but try also the white cornmeal which is milled from white corn. Corn is less nutritious by itself than many of its grain cousins.

Blue Corn: Used for both cornmeal and flour, blue corn is attributed to the Hopi Indians of the American Southwest. Blue cornmeal or flour may be used in place of any cornmeal. Blue corn is more nutritious than the yellow or white and has a subtle, sweet taste.

OATS

Rolled Oats: The grinding of oats leaves the bran and germ intact and, therefore, the nutrients. Fairly high in protein, oats are also high in vitamins B and E. Rolled oats are the most familiar form of oats to most of us. The grains are steamed, rolled into flakes and dried.

Oat Bran: Oat bran is nutritious and adds fiber to a diet. In baking of breads, oat bran will add a nice moisture to the texture.

Oat Flour: Milled or ground rolled oats. Try making your own in your food processor or blender: blend 1 cup at a time at high speed until a fine flour forms, about 1 minute. It is also available for purchase in health food stores or by mail order.

RICE

Rice Grains: Rice is no stranger to most of our dinner tables in the form of boiled grains. The most common grains found in grocery stores have had their hulls removed, hence most of their nutritional value.

Rice Flour: A low gluten flour, this must be used in conjunction with a white flour such as bread flour. Find it in the Oriental section of your grocery store or in a health food store.

Rice Bran: This has recently been discovered to have the same qualities as oat bran in lowering blood cholesterol levels. As with all bran, it is the outer layer of the kernel and has high nutritional value.

Rice Syrup: A sweetener containing no fructose or sucrose. Find it in health food stores.

RYE

Rye Flour: Milled from the rye berry or the entire kernel, rye flour has a high nutrient content. The darker the color, the stronger the taste and the nutrient value. There is no gluten in rye flours; this must be used in combination with a white flour. The larger the percentage of rye, the smaller and denser the loaf will be.

Rye Meal: A coarser grind than flour of the rye kernel.

Rye Berry: The berry or kernel of rye, as wheat berries, may be sprouted and used in its entirety in bread for the highest nutritional content.

SOY

Soybeans: A very inexpensive source of high protein, soybeans are used in many different ways and foods.

Soy Flakes: Pressed soybeans which can be added to bread for crunchy, tasty bread.

Soy Flour: High in protein and low in calories, soy flour is often added to high protein, diet-type breads. It adds moisture and is a natural preservative. Soy flour is usually added in small amounts as the taste may be found to be somewhat overpowering.

LESSER KNOWN GRAINS

Amaranth: Attributed to the Aztec Indians, amaranth is extremely high in protein, vitamins, minerals and calcium. You can find amaranth grain, cereals, etc., in your health food store and may find some in large grocery stores. The grains themselves may be cooked for a hot cereal, sprouted for salads or breads, toasted as nuts or even popped like popcorn. If you pop it, keep in mind that it may burn easily without a small amount of oil.

The history of amaranth is fascinating. When the Aztecs were conquered by the Spaniards, it was discovered that the Aztecs were mixing sacrificial blood with amaranth. In an attempt to end this practice, Cortez ordered all amaranth destroyed. It was during an archaeological expedition that some seeds were discovered and later replanted, giving us amaranth once again.

Buckwheat/Kasha: This grain has a very high protein count. It can be found in cereal form in many grocery and health food stores. Nutritionally, it is rich in vitamins B and E and has a high calcium content. Buckwheat flour is most commonly known for its use in pancakes.

Quinoa: Pronounced KEEN-wah, this is a fondly remembered grain from time I spent in Peru. Recently available in the United States, this grain is quickly catching on even though it is somewhat expensive. Extremely high in protein, (anywhere from 14 to 19 percent), quinoa is also an excellent source of calcium, and has a high lysine content, as well as vitamin C, thiamine, riboflavin and niacin. Quinoa grains may be cooked the same as rice. The flour is expensive but worth it in quinoa bread, which has a slightly nutty taste.

It also has an interesting history: Pizzaro attempted to destroy much of the crop in an effort to weaken the Incas during the conquest. As time passed, the Spaniards looked down upon quinoa as a grain for "heathens" and discounted the nutritional values. To this day, many upper-class Peruvians consider quinoa a grain suitable for the indigenous only!

HINTS AND TROUBLESHOOTING

If you have just received a bread machine and you are not sure how to use it, I strongly recommend reading two things:

1. The owner's manual which came with the machine.
2. The introductory chapters of this book.

Don't be afraid of the new machine. It really is as simple as 1-2-3-4-5:

1. Measure the ingredients and put them into the pan in the order specified (DAK and Welbilt read recipes from yeast up).
2. Choose the cycle and the setting.
3. Press the start button.
4. Check the dough after about 5 minutes of kneading to ensure that the dough has formed a round, smooth ball.

5. Remove the fully baked loaf of bread from the machine 2 to 4 hours later, depending on what machine you have.

Perhaps the single most important thing to check is the consistency of the dough after 5 to 10 minutes of kneading.

Many machines have a viewing window but if yours does not, don't be afraid to open it briefly during the kneading process. Open it long enough to check the consistency and then to make any adjustments necessary. Don't leave the lid open long and don't open it during the baking cycle.

There are variables which must be addressed whether bread is made by hand (the old fashioned way) or by machine. The flour and other ingredients pick up the moisture from the air. The moisture content of the grain berries themselves may vary as will the absorbency of whole grain flour according to how it was milled. As a result, the dough may have too much liquid, which could result in an overflow or a sunken top.

When kneading dough by hand, you develop an ability to feel the right consistency. When kneading dough by machine, you can see the right consistency. If you have problems with consistency, allow the machine to knead the dough for approximately 5 minutes and then look at the dough. With few exceptions, it should form a nice, smooth ball. Sometimes the ball will be round and other times, it may take on more of a cylindrical shape which "tornadoes" up the side of the pan.

By watching the dough on a regular basis, you will soon develop a sense for what looks right. If you stick your finger in and touch it, it should feel moist but not really be sticky. Dough which is too dry will not mix properly or it may cause the machine to struggle (you'll hear it). It may be uneven (not smooth) or have two or more balls of dough. If this is the case, simply add whatever liquid you are using, one tablespoon at a time, until the required consistency is obtained. Conversely, dough which is too wet will not be able to form a ball, and flour should be added 1 tablespoon at a time until the required consistency is obtained.

If you hear the paddle rotating, but the ingredients on top of the dough are not moving — Check to see that the paddle is inserted properly. Sometimes either the paddle was not placed on the kneading shaft correctly or it has slipped. The easiest way to check is to turn off the machine, reach in and feel whether the paddle is on correctly. It can usually just be pushed harder onto the shaft and the machine restarted without any difficulties (except for a messy hand!).

If the bread rises well but then collapses during baking —It is either rising too fast in hot weather (cut yeast, sugar and/or increase salt or use a shorter cycle) or the size of the recipe is too large (use a smaller size recipe).

Too much moisture in the dough may cause a sunken top or a mushroom. Cut back the amount of liquid by 1/4 cup and add it in slowly as the machine is kneading. Stop adding it when the dough forms a smooth round ball.

If the crust is too dark or brown —Bake on "light" if your machine has crust control. If not, try removing the bread about 5 minutes prior to the end of the baking cycle. If your machine does not tell you how much time is left, try cutting the amount of sugar (which darkens the crust). If all of these methods fail, stop the machine at the end of the first kneading cycle and start the machine over again.

Brush butter or oil on the loaf while it is still hot to soften the crust. Milk will give a softer crust than water.

If the bread is not rising and/or is doughy (not baking properly) and heavy —You should use the sweet or raisin cycle on your machine if available. Natural sugars found in fruits may actually inhibit the rising of bread and cause the bread to bake improperly. Cut down on fruits and other sugary substances. Too much butter or fat may cause a similar problem. While this may happen with any machine, it seems to happen more often with the glass-domed machines. If you have a glass-domed machine and have what I call "the doughy blues," you may also place a piece of aluminum foil on the glass dome (only) to maintain even heat. Do not block any air vents.

If the bread has large air bubbles — Cut the amount of yeast used.

Some breads may be heavy and dense just because of the ingredients. Nonwheat flours or meals such as rye, oat or corn do not contain as much gluten as wheat and will naturally be lower rising and denser than all wheat. In addition, ingredients such as wheat germ or bran actually break the gluten strands, causing breads to rise less. It may be helpful to add 1 1/2 tsp. to 2 tbs. of vital (wheat) gluten (available in health food stores) to achieve a higher rise and/or a better texture when using large amounts of such grains. Other reasons for breads not rising include a large amount of salt which inhibits rising and/or not enough sugar or water.

Sometimes raisins or similar ingredients do not mix into the dough evenly.

Any dried fruit may be lightly floured to prevent pieces from sticking to each other. You may also add ingredients at the beginning of the second kneading cycle. For variety, try using Craisins (dried, sweetened cranberries) as a substitute for raisins.

MEASUREMENT EQUIVALENTS

1/3 tsp.	=	heaping 1/4 tsp.
2/3 tsp.	=	heaping 1/2 tsp. or scant 3/4 tsp.
1 tsp.	=	1/3 tbs.
1 1/2 tsp.	=	1/2 tbs.
3 tsp.	=	1 tbs.
4 tsp.	=	1 1/3 tbs.
1/3 tbs.	=	1 tsp.
1/2 tbs.	=	1 1/2 tsp.
1 tbs.	=	3 tsp.
1 1/3 tsp.	=	4 tsp. or 1 tbs. plus 1 tsp.
1/8 cup	=	1 fluid oz. or 2 tbs.
1/4 cup	=	2 fluid oz. or 4 tbs.
1/3 cup	=	2 2/3 fluid oz. or 5 1/3 tbs.
3/8 cup	=	3 fluid oz., 6 tbs. or 1/4 cup plus 2 tbs.
1/2 cup	=	4 fluid oz. or 8 tbs.
5/8 cup	=	5 fluid oz. or 1/2 cup plus 2 tbs.
2/3 cup	=	5 1/3 fluid oz. or 10 2/3 tbs.
3/4 cup	=	6 fluid oz. or 12 tbs.
7/8 cup	=	7 fluid oz. or 3/4 cup plus 2 tbs.
1 cup	=	8 fluid oz., 16 tbs. or 48 tsp.

GENERAL HINTS

- If breads don't rise consistently, try moving the machine to ensure that it is not in a draft.
- If that doesn't work, try using bottled water instead of tap water.
- If storing flour in the refrigerator, bring to room temperature or put on at least a 20-minute timer to allow it to come to room temperature. Cold ingredients will cause the bread to not rise as well – it kills the yeast.
- If your machine does not have a preheat cycle, warm milk, water or other liquid in a microwave for about one minute, or until it feels warm to the inside of your wrist (like a baby bottle). Cut butter or margarine into quarters for better and easier distribution. Butter and eggs may be used straight from the refrigerator or room temperature.
- If measuring honey, maple syrup, molasses or similar sweeteners, measure the oil first. By using the oiled measuring spoon the honey, etc. will simply slide right off the spoon! You'll notice that all recipes using honey, etc. use oil instead of butter–for this very reason.
- Bananas should be very ripe and should be mashed or cut into small, 1-inch slices.
- Cheese should be lightly packed in the measuring cup.
- If making breads that rely on cheese, fruits or sour cream as a main source of liquid, do not use the timer and watch the dough carefully for moisture content. Add water or flour one tablespoon at a time after 5 minutes of kneading to ensure a proper texture. If desired, after dough has kneaded into a ball, stop the machine and restart it.

- Cut butter or margarine into pieces for better and easier distribution. Butter and eggs may be added while cold or at room temperature.

GETTING THE MOST FROM YOUR BREAD MACHINE

You can make some delicious meals or snacks from leftover bread or from the dough. Here are some other ideas for using your bread machine, including gift ideas. For more ideas, see my books: *Entrees from Your Bread Machine, Edible Pockets for Every Meal, The Best Pizza Is Made at Home,* and *New Recipes for Your Sandwich Maker.*

OVERNIGHT DOUGH

Making breakfast breads on a timer is a very simple task. However, making dough in the evening for hot coffee rolls in the morning is also very simple and not as time consuming as you would think. Recommended recipes: *Brioche*, page 129, *Almond Butter Crescents* (and variations), page 132, *Cinnamon Rolls*, page 135, *Sweet Rolls, page* 136, or *Lithuanian Coffee Bread, page* 140. Note that *Crusty Pizza Dough*, page 145 may be made with a cold rise also.

Place ingredients in machine and start the dough cycle in the normal manner. As soon as the machine has completed the first kneading and the dough is a nice, round, smooth ball, stop the machine. Depending on the pan itself or the space in the refrigerator, remove the pan, cover with plastic wrap and refrigerate overnight. Otherwise, remove the dough and place in a greased bowl or a (large) floured plastic bag (leaving room to expand); place in the refrigerator overnight. The chilled dough will rise slowly through the night. Remove the dough in the morning, let sit for 5 to 10 minutes and then roll or shape according to directions. Let rise the second time in the normal fashion and bake according to recipe directions.

DINNER BREAD BOWLS

Soup/Chili Bowls are a wonderful use of bread on those cold, wet (rain or snow) days when you are home. Use your favorite dough to complement your hearty stew, bean soup, or chili. A 2-cup recipe makes 2 to 3 bowls, a 3-cup recipe makes 4 to 5 bowls and a 4-cup recipe makes 6 to 7 bowls.

Make the dough on the dough cycle. Upon completion of the cycle, remove dough and break into desired number of bread bowls. Shape each piece into large rolls or balls. Place on a lightly greased baking sheet, cover and let rise for 1 to 1½ hours. The "rolls" will be quite large. Bake in a preheated 350° oven for 20 to 25 minutes or until golden brown. Place each "bowl" in a real bowl, cut off the top and scoop out the inside. Fill with stew or chili and serve with or without the top.

BREAD WREATHS

One of our favorite Christmas gifts, which we give to teachers, friends and neighbors, is a bread wreath. Make dough on the dough cycle. Upon completion of the cycle, remove dough and divide into 10 to 15 balls. Roll each ball into a roll shape and place each roll on the outer rim of a lightly greased pizza pan (disposable if you are giving them away) so that they touch each other slightly. Cover and let rise for about 30 minutes. Bake in a preheated

350° oven for 18 to 20 minutes.

BAKING WITH KIDS

Whether you have young children, grandchildren or visiting children, baking with young preschoolers is a great way to have special time and teach them too. Let the children help you measure the ingredients and pour them into the pan — they'll begin learning basic math skills including fractions! When the bread is hot, they'll have a feeling of accomplishment – like they have made the bread by themselves. In addition to simply making the bread, try some of the following:

Put food coloring in the bread – "big, beautiful blue bread," red for Christmas or Valentines Day, etc. Green does not do well, but yellow, red and blue do.

Let the children roll out pizza dough – does it really matter what shape it is? Then, if you are really brave, let them make their own pizza.

Let the children shape rolls – just like Play Dough (I wonder where the name came from?) Somehow sandwiches taste better when they made the bread...

PIZZA PARTY

Some of our best casual dinner parties have been pizza parties. Depending on the group, I have asked each person or couple to bring 1/2 to 1 lb. of cheese and a prepared, favorite pizza topping. Other times, I have provided all the ingredients – it just depends on the group and the reason for the party. Usually, I make several batches of dough and I will roll it out, and give it to a person or couple to choose a sauce, cheese and toppings. As one couple is making theirs, another couple's pizza is cooking.

To make multiple dough recipes: 1) Add ingredients to the machine in the normal method and start machine on dough cycle. As soon as the machine has finished the first kneading and the dough is a smooth, round ball, stop the machine and remove the dough from the pan. Place the dough in a lightly greased bowl, cover and let rise for 1 to 1½ hours. Then load machine up with the second batch of dough. If desired, the covered bowl may be placed in the refrigerator and the dough allowed to cold-rise for 6 to 8 hours. Remove dough from refrigerator about 15 minutes before rolling out.

Pizza pans – Small, individual pizza screens may be purchased quite cheaply at restaurant supply stores. I do use a pizza stone but usually put the pan on the stone until the pizza is firm enough to slide off onto the stone directly. A cheaters way to get that stone baking without the mess of sliding the dough onto the stone!

LEFTOVER BREAD IDEAS

Yes, it does occasionally happen that you may have leftover breads. Once the ducks and birds have been fed, what do you do with it? Here is a simple list of ideas: croutons, bread crackers, garlic bread, bread stuffing, bread salad, egg strata (may be served for breakfast or dinner), cheese fondue or — of course — bread puddings.

WHITE AND CHEESE BREADS

WHITE BREAD

This is a very rich bread — terrific for sandwiches. You'll find yourself going back for more and more. It is not, however, one of the more dietetic. Well worth the calories anyway! Use an egg white, egg yolk or 2 tbs. egg substitute for 1/2 egg.

	Small	**Medium**	**Large**
water	1/2 cup	3/4 cup	1 cup
margarine or butter	2 tbs.	2 1/2 tbs.	3 tbs.
egg	1/2	1	1
sugar	1 1/2 tbs.	2 tbs.	2 tbs.
salt	3/4 tsp.	1 tsp.	1 1/2 tsp.
bread flour	2 cups	3 cups	3 1/2 cups
nonfat dry milk	2 1/2 tbs.	1/4 cup	1/3 cup
yeast	1 tsp.	1 1/2 tsp.	2 tsp.
Flour equivalent	*2 cups*	*3 cups*	*3 1/2 cups*
Cycle	*basic cycle, no timer (eggs)*		
Setting	*medium*		

VARIATION: Add 1 tsp. 1 1/2 tsp. or 2 tsp. seeds such as caraway, anise, dill, fennel, flax or sesame. It will be just enough to give a little extra flavor but not enough to overpower.

SALLY LUNN

This very rich English bread is loaded with butter and eggs and is not dietetic by any means! Make the 1½ lb. size in glass-domed machines. Set the machine for a light crust. The eggs give it lots of terrific taste and color. Tradition says that a young Englishwoman, Sally Lunn, sold this bread on the streets of Bath. Most bread cookbooks contain a version of this, which attests to its wonderful flavor. This is one of those breads which will never last to see leftovers.

	Small	**Medium**	**Large**
milk	½ cup	⅔ cup	¾ cup
margarine or butter	3 tbs.	4 tbs.	4 tbs.
eggs	1	2	2
salt	1 tsp.	1½ tsp.	2 tsp.
sugar	2½ tbs.	¼ cup	⅓ cup
bread flour	2 cups	3 cups	3½ cups
yeast	1 tsp.	1½ tsp.	2 tsp.
Flour equivalent	*2 cups*	*3 cups*	*3½ cups*
Cycle	*sweet or basic cycle, no timer (eggs)*		
Setting	*light*		

PORTUGUESE SWEET BREAD

Maria and Manuel, from Portugal, are living here while Manuel completes his doctoral degree. She has experimented with recipes to closely resemble those of her country. This is one of my favorites.

	Small	**Medium**	**Large**
milk	1/2 cup	3/4 cup	7/8 cup
eggs	1	1	2
margarine or butter	1 tbs.	1 1/2 tbs.	2 tbs.
sugar	3 tbs.	1/4 cup	1/3 cup
salt	1/2 tsp.	3/4 tsp.	1 tsp.
bread flour	2 cups	2 1/2 cups	3 cups
yeast	1 tsp.	1 1/2 tsp.	2 tsp.
Flour equivalent	*2 cups*	*2 1/2 cups*	*3 cups*
Cycle	*sweet or basic cycle, no timer (eggs)*		
Setting	*light or medium*		

VARIATIONS: Add 1 tsp., 1 1/2 tsp. or 2 tsp. grated lemon zest or grated nutmeg with the dry ingredients.

PORTUGUESE WHITE BREAD

A very light-colored, airy bread. Slightly difficult to cut while hot — but who can wait until it cools?

	Small	**Medium**	**Large**
water	3/4 cup	1 cup	1 1/4 cups
margarine or butter	2 tbs.	3 tbs.	1/4 cup
sugar	2 tsp.	1 tbs.	1 tbs.
salt	3/4 tsp.	1 tsp.	1 1/2 tsp.
bread flour	2 cups	3 cups	3 1/2 cups
yeast	1 tsp.	1 1/2 tsp.	2 tsp.
Flour equivalent	*2 cups*	*3 cups*	*3 1/2 cups*
Cycle	*basic cycle, timer*		
Setting	*medium*		

ENGLISH MUFFIN BREAD

This is a really good, easy way to get that English muffin taste and texture. Great bread to set on the timer for a hot breakfast bread. In order to have the proper texture, there may be a sunken top to this bread.

	Small	**Medium**	**Large**
water	7/8 cup	1 1/4 cups	1 1/2 cups
sugar	1 1/2 tsp.	2 tsp.	1 tbs.
salt	3/4 tsp.	1 tsp.	1 tsp.
baking soda	1/8 tsp.	1/4 tsp.	1/2 tsp.
bread flour	2 cups	3 cups	3 1/2 cups
nonfat dry milk	2 tbs.	3 tbs.	1/4 cup
yeast	1 tsp.	1 1/2 tsp.	2 tsp.
Flour equivalent	*2 cups*	*3 cups*	*3 1/2 cups*
Cycle	*basic cycle, timer*		
Setting	*medium*		

PEASANT BREAD

This recipe is based on one given to me by Carmen, a friend and neighbor. It's a very moist, chewy bread with a light, crispy crust. Absolutely wonderful with butter or cheese. It is somewhat similar to English Muffin Bread but more moist. The dough will appear wet. This makes great baguettes by using the dough cycle. See page 127 for directions.

	Small	Medium	Large
water	7/8 cup	1 1/3 cups	1 1/2 cups
sugar	1 1/2 tsp.	2 tsp.	1 tbs.
salt	3/4 tsp.	1 tsp.	1 tsp.
bread flour	2 cups	3 cups	3 1/2 cups
yeast	1 1/2 tsp.	2 tsp.	2 1/2 tsp.
Flour equivalent	*2 cups*	*3 cups*	*3 1/2 cups*
Cycle	*basic cycle, timer*		
Setting	*medium*		

SOUR CREAM BREAD

Great sandwich bread with a nice texture and great taste. Warm the sour cream. Adjust the consistency with water as necessary and scrape the sides of the pan with a rubber spatula if you need to. As with any recipe with dairy products, do not use the timer.

	Small	**Medium**	**Large**
water	2 tbs.	$2\frac{1}{2}$ tbs.	3 tbs.
sour cream	1 cup	$1\frac{1}{3}$ cups	$1\frac{3}{4}$ cups
salt	$\frac{1}{2}$ tsp.	$\frac{3}{4}$ tsp.	1 tsp.
baking soda	$\frac{1}{8}$ tsp.	$\frac{1}{4}$ tsp.	$\frac{1}{2}$ tsp.
sugar	1 tbs.	$1\frac{1}{2}$ tbs.	2 tbs.
bread flour	$2\frac{1}{2}$ cups	$3\frac{1}{3}$ cups	4 cups
yeast	$1\frac{1}{2}$ tsp.	2 tsp.	2 tsp.
Flour equivalent	*$2\frac{1}{2}$ cups*	*$3\frac{1}{3}$ cups*	*4 cups*

Cycle — *basic cycle, no timer (dairy products, watch consistency)*

Setting — *medium*

CRUSTY CUBAN BREAD

This ethnic bread is very similar to a French or Italian Bread. It tends to be low-rising due to the lack of fat and small amount of sugar. Keep an eye on the dough and add a tablespoon or two of water if the dough looks dry or if the machine sounds like it is struggling. To use this recipe for bread bowls with a hearty stew, see page 26. This makes great baguettes by using the dough cycle. See page 127 for directions.

	Small	Medium	Large
water	3/4 cup	1 1/4 cups	1 1/2 cups
sugar	1 tsp.	1 1/2 tsp.	2 tsp.
salt	3/4 tsp.	1 tsp.	1 tsp.
bread flour	2 cups	3 cups	3 1/2 cups
yeast	1 1/2 tsp.	2 tsp.	2 1/2 tsp.
Flour equivalent	*2 cups*	*3 cups*	*3 1/2 cups*
Cycle	*basic cycle, no timer (watch consistency)*		
Setting	*medium*		

FRENCH HONEY BREAD

This wonderful, slightly sweet French bread is lightly colored with a light, crispy crust. Expect a high-rising loaf. Measure the oil first, then the honey. This makes great baguettes by using the dough cycle. See page 127 for directions.

	Small	**Medium**	**Large**
water	3/4 cup	1 1/8 cups	1 1/4 cups
olive oil	2 tsp.	1 tbs.	1 1/2 tbs.
honey	2 tsp.	1 tbs.	1 1/2 tbs.
salt	1/2 tsp.	3/4 tsp.	1 tsp.
sugar	3/4 tsp.	1 tsp.	1 1/2 tsp.
bread flour	2 cups	3 cups	3 1/2 cups
yeast	1 1/2 tsp.	2 tsp.	2 1/2 tsp.
Flour equivalent	*2 cups*	*3 cups*	*3 1/2 cups*
Cycle	*basic cycle, timer*		
Setting	*medium*		

ITALIAN BREAD

This is perfect bread with an Italian meal. Do not use the timer as you must watch the consistency of the dough and add water if necessary. To use this recipe for bread bowls with a hearty stew, see page 26. See page 127 for directions on using this recipe in a traditional, ethnic shape using the dough cycle.

	Small	**Medium**	**Large**
water	7/8 cup	1 1/4 cups	1 1/2 cups
sugar	1 tsp.	1 1/2 tsp.	2 tsp.
salt	1/4 tsp.	1/2 tsp.	3/4 tsp.
bread flour	2 cups	3 cups	3 1/2 cups
yeast	1 1/2 tsp.	2 tsp.	2 1/2 tsp.
Flour equivalent	*2 cups*	*3 cups*	*3 1/2 cups*
Cycle	*basic cycle, no timer (watch consistency)*		
Setting	*medium*		

BUTTERMILK BREAD

You get great taste and texture and a light, fluffy bread without fresh buttermilk.

	Small	**Medium**	**Large**
water	2/3 cup	1 cup	1 1/4 cups
margarine or butter	1 tbs.	2 tbs.	2 tbs.
sugar	1 tsp.	1 1/2 tsp.	2 tsp.
salt	1/2 tsp.	3/4 tsp.	1 tsp.
bread flour	2 cups	3 cups	3 1/2 cups
buttermilk powder	3 tbs.	1/4 cup	1/3 cup
yeast	1 1/2 tsp.	2 tsp.	2 1/2 tsp.
Flour equivalent	*2 cups*	*3 cups*	*3 1/2 cups*
Cycle	*basic cycle, timer*		
Setting	*medium*		

AUSTRIAN MALT BREAD

Use 2 tbs., 3 tbs. or 1/4 cup malted milk powder instead of the buttermilk powder. It can be found in the dry milk section of large grocery stores. The malt gives the bread an interesting flavor.

COTTAGE CHEESE BREAD

Warm the cottage cheese in the microwave for a minute or so. Watch the consistency and add water as necessary. Use an egg white or yolk or 2 tbs. egg substitute for ½ egg.

	Small	**Medium**	**Large**
water	3–4 tbs.	3–4 tbs.	¼–⅓ cup
cottage cheese	⅔ cup	¾ cup	1 cup
margarine or butter	1½ tbs.	1½ tbs.	2 tbs.
egg	½	1	1
sugar	2 tsp.	1 tbs.	1 tbs.
baking soda	⅛ tsp.	¼ tsp.	¼ tsp.
salt	¾ tsp.	1 tsp.	1 tsp.
bread flour	2 cups	2½ cups	3 cups
yeast	1½ tsp.	2 tsp.	2 tsp.
Flour equivalent	*2 cups*	*3 cups*	*3½ cups*
Cycle	*sweet or basic cycle, no timer (dairy products, watch consistency)*		
Setting	*medium*		

DILL BREAD – This is wonderful with either pasta or fish. Add 2 tsp., 1 tbs. or 1½ tbs. dried dill weed to the above recipe.

RICOTTA BREAD

This made a huge hit with friends and tasters who ranked it one of the best. It slices very well. Use an egg white, yolk or 2 tbs. egg substitute for 1/2 egg. Warm the cheese for a high rise, but puncture the dough on the second rise if it rises too high.

	Small	**Medium**	**Large**
milk	1/4 cup	1/3 cup	1/2 cup
ricotta cheese	1 cup	1 1/3 cups	1 1/2 cups
margarine or butter	2 tbs.	2 1/2 tbs.	3 tbs.
eggs	1/2	1	1
sugar	2 1/2 tbs.	1/4 cup	1/3 cup
salt	1 tsp.	1 tsp.	1 1/2 tsp.
bread flour	2 cups	3 cups	3 1/2 cups
yeast	1 tsp.	1 1/2 tsp.	2 tsp.
Flour equivalent	*2 cups*	*3 cups*	*3 1/2 cups*
Cycle	*sweet or basic cycle, no timer (dairy products, watch consistency)*		
Setting	*medium*		

HERB RICOTTA BREAD: Add 2 tsp., 1 tbs. Or 1 1/2 tbs. of a dried herb (basil, oregano or parsley).

CREAM CHEESE BREAD

This is more of a dessert bread or cake, which makes great toast with preserves or French toast. Bring the cream cheese to room temperature for several hours or warm in the microwave. Scrape sides of pan if necessary and adjust the consistency with milk or water if you need to.

	Small	**Medium**	**Large**
milk	1/3 cup	1/3 cup	1/2 cup
cream cheese	4 oz	6 oz	8 oz.
margarine or butter	2 tbs.	2 1/2 tbs.	3 tbs.
egg	1/2	1	1
sugar	2 tbs.	3 tbs.	3 tbs.
salt	3/4 tsp.	1 tsp.	1 1/2 tsp.
bread flour	2 cups	3 cups	3 1/2 cups
yeast	1 tsp.	1 1/2 tsp.	2 tsp.
Flour equivalent	*2 cups*	*3 cups*	*3 1/2 cups*
Cycle	*sweet or basic cycle, no timer (dairy products, watch consistency)*		
Setting	*medium*		

CHEDDAR CHEESE BREAD

This is a delicious bread. Use grated or shredded cheddar cheese and lightly pack it into the cup. The cheese may affect the consistency of the dough, so keep an eye on it and adjust the moisture if you need to.

	Small	Medium	Large
water or milk	2/3 cup	1 cup	1 1/4 cups
margarine or butter	1 tbs.	1 tbs.	1 1/2 tbs.
cheddar cheese, shredded	1/2 cup	2/3 cup	3/4 cup
sugar	2 tsp.	1 tbs.	1 1/2 tbs.
salt	1/2 tsp.	3/4 tsp.	1 tsp.
bread flour	2 cups	3 cups	3 1/2 cups
yeast	1 tsp.	1 1/2 tsp.	2 tsp.
Flour equivalent	*2 cups*	*3 cups*	*3 1/2 cups*
Cycle	*sweet or basic cycle, no timer (dairy products, watch consistency)*		
Setting	*medium*		

WHOLE WHEAT, GRAIN AND CEREAL BREADS

Because whole grains tend to be lower rising and denser, some recipes use higher amounts of flour than normal. If you have difficulty with whole wheat or whole grain loaves, allow the machine to knead one time and then turn off the machine and start it again, producing a longer kneading time. If you do not have a whole wheat cycle on your machine but do have a sweet cycle, try using the sweet cycle or the basic for whole grain breads.

Many of the ingredients used in these loaves (rolled wheat flakes, wheat germ, bulgur wheat, etc.) may be found in either the cereal or natural foods section of large grocery stores, or in natural or health food stores. Items such as seeds (flax, sesame, etc) are far cheaper bought in bulk from these stores than in the spice section of the grocery store.

WHOLE WHEAT

This is my favorite whole wheat. It's a high-rising bread that slices very well.

	Small	**Medium**	**Large**
water	1/2 cup	3/4 cup	1 1/4 cups
margarine or butter	2 tbs.	3 tbs.	1/4 cup
egg	1	1	1
sugar	1 1/2 tbs.	2 tbs.	2 1/2 tbs.
salt	3/4 tsp.	1 tsp.	1 1/2 tsp.
bread flour	1 1/2 cups	2 cups	2 2/3 cups
whole wheat flour	3/4 cup	1 cup	1 1/3 cups
yeast	1 tsp.	1 1/2 tsp.	2 tsp.
Flour equivalent	*2 cups*	*3 cups*	*4 cups*
Cycle	*whole wheat, sweet or basic cycle, timer*		
Setting	*medium*		

VARIATION: Add 1 tsp. 1 1/2 tsp. or 2 tsp. seeds such as caraway, anise, dill, fennel, flax or sesame. It will be just enough to give a little extra flavor but not enough to overpower.

SPROUT BREAD

This is worth the trouble of sprouting the berries. The sprouts affect the amount of liquid required and you will have to adjust the consistency with water or flour.

	Small	**Medium**	**Large**
water	2/3 cup	3/4 cup	1 cup
margarine or butter	1 1/2 tbs.	2 tbs.	2 1/2 tbs.
sugar	2 tsp.	1 tbs.	1 1/2 tbs.
salt	1/2 tsp.	3/4 tsp.	1 tsp.
sprouted wheat berries	1/3 cup	1/2 cup	2/3 cup
bread flour	2 cups	2 1/2 cups	3 cups
yeast	1 tsp.	1 1/2 tsp.	2 1/2 tsp.

Two to three days prior to making this bread, place 1/3 to 1/2 cup wheat berries in a sprouting jar (or any glass jar with cheesecloth tied down with a rubber band). Cover with water and allow to sit overnight (at least 12 hours). Drain and rinse again, right through the screen or cheesecloth, and set the jar mouth-side down at a 45° angle in a warm, dark place. Rinse sprouts twice a day. They are ready for use when you see small sprouts of about 1/8 to 1/4 inch. (Wheat berry sprouts should be no longer than the berry itself.)

Flour equivalent	*2 1/3 cups*	*3 cups*	*3 2/3 cups*
Cycle	*whole wheat, sweet or basic cycle, no timer (check consistency)*		
Setting	*medium*		

NINE-GRAIN BREAD

Nine-grain cereal consists of cracked wheat, barley, corn, millet, oats, triticale, brown rice, soya and flax seed and is available for purchase either in bulk or pre-boxed. It may be carried in a large grocery store or a natural food store. Seven-grain cereal may be used as a substitute. Some stores carry one and not the other.

	Small	**Medium**	**Large**
water	1 cup	1 1/3 cups	1 1/2 cups
margarine or butter	2 tbs.	2 1/2 tbs.	3 tbs.
brown sugar	1 1/2 tbs.	2 tbs.	2 1/2 tbs.
salt	1 tsp.	1 tsp.	1 tsp.
9-grain cereal	1 cup	1 1/3 cups	1 1/2 cups
bread flour	2 cups	2 2/3 cups	3 cups
yeast	1 tsp.	1 1/2 tsp.	2 tsp.
Flour equivalent	*3 cups*	*4 cups*	*4 1/2 cups*
Cycle	*whole wheat, sweet or basic cycle, timer*		
Setting	*medium*		

CRACKED WHEAT BREAD

One of the best. This natural, great-tasting and high-rising bread has a bit of crunchiness. If in doubt about the size to make, make the smallest size.

	Small	**Medium**	**Large**
water	1 cup	1 1/4 cups	1 1/2 cups
cracked wheat	1/3 cup	1/2 cup	2/3 cup
vegetable oil	1 1/2 tbs.	2 tbs.	2 1/2 tbs.
honey	1 tbs.	1 tbs.	1 1/2 tbs.
salt	1/2 tsp.	1 tsp.	1 tsp.
whole wheat flour	3/4 cup	1 cup	1 1/3 cups
bread flour	1 cup	1 1/2 cups	2 cups
vital gluten, optional	1 tbs.	2 tbs.	2 tbs.
yeast	1 tsp.	1 1/2 tsp.	2 tsp.

Allow the cracked wheat to sit in the measured liquid at least 1 hour. Add the water and cracked wheat with the liquid ingredients. Adjust the consistency with additional water or flour.

Flour equivalent	*2 cups*	*3 cups*	*4 cups*
Cycle	*whole wheat, sweet or basic cycle, timer*		
Setting	*medium*		

HIGH PROTEIN DIET (CORNELL) BREAD

This is a tasty, dense loaf. The recipe is based on a formula devised for superior nutrition in bread by Cornell University. Wheat germ, soy flour and nonfat dry milk are added to each cup of flour in the Cornell Formula; this recipe makes it easier.

	Small	**Medium**	**Large**
water	1 cup	1 1/4 cups	1 1/2 cups
vegetable oil	1 tbs.	1 1/2 tbs.	2 tbs.
honey	1 tbs.	1 1/2 tbs.	2 tbs.
salt	3/4 tsp.	1 tsp.	1 tsp.
wheat germ	2 tbs.	3 tbs.	1/4 cup
soy flour	1/4 cup	1/3 cup	1/2 cup
whole wheat flour	1 cup	1 1/3 cups	1 2/3 cups
bread flour	1 1/2 cups	1 2/3 cups	2 cups
nonfat dry milk	1/4 cup	1/3 cup	1/2 cup
vital gluten, optional	1 1/2 tsp.	2 tsp.	1 tbs.
yeast	1 1/2 tsp.	2 tsp.	2 1/2 tsp.
Flour equivalent	*3 cups*	*4 cups*	*5 cups*
Cycle	*whole wheat, sweet or basic cycle, timer*		
Setting	*medium*		

BRAN BREAD

This wonderfully hearty bread is so healthy! Wheat bran is also known as millers' bran, and like oat bran, can be found in health food stores. Yes, the salt is the same amount for all sizes!

	Small	**Medium**	**Large**
water	1 cup	1 1/3 cups	1 1/2 cups
margarine or butter	2 tbs.	2 1/2 tbs.	3 tbs.
brown sugar	1 tbs.	1 1/2 tbs.	2 tbs.
salt	1 tsp.	1 tsp.	1 tsp.
wheat germ	1/4 cup	1/3 cup	1/2 cup
whole wheat flour	1/2 cup	2/3 cup	3/4 cup
oat or wheat bran	1 cup	1 1/3 cups	1 1/2 cups
bread flour	1 1/2 cups	2 cups	2 1/2 cups
vital gluten, optional	1 1/2 tsp.	2 tsp.	1 tbs.
yeast	1 1/2 tsp.	2 tsp.	2 1/2 tsp.
Flour equivalent	*3 1/4 cups*	*4 1/3 cups*	*5 1/4 cups*
Cycle	*whole wheat, sweet or basic cycle, timer*		
Setting	*medium*		

MULTI-GRAIN BREAD

This hearty, somewhat dense, full-of-fiber bread is wonderful with stew or soup. You can substitute cracked wheat for bulgur. Scrape sides of pan with a rubber spatula if necessary.

	Small	**Medium**	**Large**
water	1 1/8 cups	1 1/3 cups	1 1/2 cups
vegetable oil	1 1/2 tbs.	2 tbs.	2 1/2 tbs.
honey	2 tbs.	2 1/2 tbs.	3 tbs.
salt	3/4 tsp.	1 tsp.	1 1/2 tsp.
bulgur wheat	1/4 cup	1/3 cup	1/2 cup
wheat germ	2 tbs.	3 tbs.	1/4 cup
wheat or oat bran	1/2 cup	2/3 cup	3/4 cup
rye flour	1/2 cup	2/3 cup	3/4 cup
rolled oats	1/4 cup	1/3 cup	1/2 cup
bread flour	1 1/2 cups	2 1/4 cups	2 1/2 cups
vital gluten	1 1/2 tbs.	2 tbs.	2 tbs.
yeast	1 1/2 tsp.	2 tsp.	2 1/2 tsp.
Flour equivalent	*3 cups*	*4 1/2 cups*	*5 1/4 cups*
Cycle	*whole wheat, sweet or basic cycle, no timer*		
Setting	*medium*		

WHEAT FLAKE BREAD

The wheat flakes, similar to oat flakes, give it a nice texture along with being nutritious. Expect a high-rising loaf.

	Small	Medium	Large
water	3/4 cup	1 1/8 cups	1 1/3 cups
margarine or butter	1 tbs.	2 tbs.	2 1/2 tbs.
brown sugar	2 tsp.	1 tbs.	1 1/2 tbs.
salt	1/4 tsp.	1/2 tsp.	3/4 tsp.
rolled wheat flakes	1/3 cup	1/2 cup	2/3 cup
whole wheat flour	2/3 cup	1 cup	1 1/3 cups
bread flour	1 cup	1 1/2 cups	2 cups
vital gluten, optional	2 tsp.	1 tbs.	1 tbs.
yeast	1 1/2 tsp.	2 tsp.	2 1/2 tsp.
Flour equivalent	*2 cups*	*3 cups*	*4 cups*
Cycle	*whole wheat, sweet or basic cycle, timer*		
Setting	*medium*		

WHEAT GERM SESAME BREAD

This high-rising bread is light and airy. Use an egg yolk or white, or 2 tbs. egg substitute, for ½ egg. During the second rise, puncture the dough if necessary, or make a smaller size. Substitute anise or fennel seeds for variety.

	Small	**Medium**	**Large**
water	2/3 cup	1 cup	1 1/4 cups
vegetable oil	2 tbs.	2 1/2 tbs.	3 tbs.
honey	2 tbs.	2 1/2 tbs.	3 tbs.
eggs	1/2	1	1
salt	1/2 tsp.	3/4 tsp.	1 tsp.
wheat germ	2 tbs.	3 tbs.	1/4 cup
sesame seeds	1 tbs.	1 1/2 tbs.	2 tbs.
whole wheat flour	3/4 cup	1 cup	1 1/4 cups
bread flour	1 1/2 cups	2 cups	2 1/2 cups
yeast	1 tsp.	1 1/2 tsp.	2 tsp.
Flour equivalent	*2 2/3 cups*	*3 1/4 cups*	*5 cups*
Cycle	*whole wheat, sweet or basic cycle, no timer (eggs)*		
Setting	*medium*		

WHOLE WHEAT OATMEAL BREAD

This great, wholesome bread slices well. It's one of my favorites. Use egg white, yolk or 2 tbs. egg substitute for the ½ egg.

	Small	Medium	Large
water	⅔ cup	1 cup	1⅓ cups
margarine or butter	2 tbs.	2 tbs.	3 tbs.
eggs	½	1	1
sugar	1½ tbs.	2 tbs.	3 tbs.
salt	½ tsp.	¾ tsp.	1 tsp.
rolled oats	⅓ cup	½ cup	⅔ cup
wheat germ	3 tbs.	¼ cup	⅓ cup
whole wheat flour	½ cup	¾ cup	1 cup
bread flour	1½ cups	2 cups	3 cups
yeast	1½ tsp.	2 tsp.	2½ tsp.
Flour equivalent	*2½ cups*	*3½ cups*	*5 cups*
Cycle	*whole wheat, sweet or basic cycle, no timer (eggs)*		
Setting	*medium*		

OATMEAL BREAD

A terrific oatmeal loaf! Regular dry milk may be substituted for buttermilk powder.

	Small	Medium	Large
water	3/4 cup	7/8 cup	1 1/3 cups
margarine or butter	2 tbs.	2 1/2 tbs.	3 tbs.
sugar	1 1/2 tbs.	2 tbs.	3 tbs.
salt	1/2 tsp.	3/4 tsp.	1 tsp.
rolled oats	2/3 cup	1 cup	1 1/3 cups
bread flour	1 1/2 cups	2 cups	3 cups
buttermilk powder	3 tbs.	1/4 cup	1/3 cup
yeast	1 1/2 tsp.	2 tsp.	2 1/2 tsp.
Flour equivalent	*2 cups*	*3 cups*	*4 cups*
Cycle	*whole wheat, sweet or basic cycle, timer*		
Setting	*medium*		

CINNAMON OATMEAL BREAD

Add 1 tsp., 1 1/2 tsp. or 2 tsp. cinnamon.

RAISIN OATMEAL BREAD

Add 1/4 cup, 1/3 cup or 1/2 cup raisins or Craisins with or without cinnamon (above).

HONEY NUT OATMEAL BREAD

While many grocery stores carry a honey nut oatmeal bread for sandwiches, this seems more of a dessert-type bread to me. Absolutely delicious and a "must try." Walnut oil may be found in some large grocery stores.

	Small	**Medium**	**Large**
water	2/3 cup	1 cup	1 1/3 cups
vegetable or walnut oil	1 tbs.	2 tbs.	3 tbs.
honey	1 tbs.	2 tbs.	3 tbs.
salt	1/2 tsp.	1 tsp.	1 tsp.
rolled oats	2/3 cup	1 cup	1 1/3 cups
whole wheat flour	1/3 cup	1/2 cup	2/3 cup
bread flour	1 cup	1 1/2 cups	2 cups
yeast	1 tsp.	1 1/2 tsp.	2 1/2 tsp.
At beep add: (If National or Panasonic, add following first kneading)			
chopped walnuts	1/3 cup	1/2 cup	2/3 cup
Flour equivalent	*2 1/3 cups*	*3 1/2 cups*	*4 2/3 cups*
Cycle	*whole wheat, sweet or basic cycle, timer*		
Setting	*medium*		

ALMOND OATMEAL BREAD

This is a wonderful, tasty bread. The almonds combined with the oats creates a delightful chewiness and a touch of crunch.

	Small	Medium	Large
milk	7/8 cup	1 1/8 cups	1 1/3 cups
margarine	2 tbs.	2 1/2 tbs.	3 tbs.
almond paste	1 1/2 tbs.	2 tbs.	2 1/2 tbs.
almond extract	1 1/2 tsp.	2 tsp.	1 tbs.
sugar	1 1/2 tsp.	2 tsp.	1 tbs.
salt	3/4 tsp.	1 tsp.	1 tsp.
rolled oats	1 cup	1 1/3 cups	1 1/2 cups
bread flour	2 cups	2 2/3 cups	3 cups
yeast	1 1/2 tsp.	2 tsp.	2 1/2 tsp.
At beep add: (If National or Panasonic, add following first kneading)			
slivered almonds	1/4 cup	1/3 cup	1/2 cup
Flour equivalent	*3 1/4 cups*	*4 1/3 cups*	*5 cups*
Cycle	*whole wheat, sweet or basic cycle, no timer (milk)*		
Setting	*medium*		

OATMEAL SESAME BREAD

This delicious sweet bread is another good choice for breakfast.

	Small	**Medium**	**Large**
water	3/4 cup	1 cup	1 1/3 cups
margarine or butter	1 tbs.	1 1/2 tbs.	2 tbs.
brown sugar	1 tbs.	1 1/2 tbs.	2 tbs.
cinnamon, optional	1/2 tsp.	3/4 tsp.	1 tsp.
salt	1/2 tsp.	3/4 tsp.	1 tsp.
sesame seeds	3 tbs.	1/4 cup	1/3 cup
rolled oats	1/3 cup	1/2 cup	2/3 cup
whole wheat flour	1/3 cup	1/2 cup	2/3 cup
bread flour	1 1/2 cups	2 cups	2 2/3 cups
yeast	1 tsp.	1 1/2 tsp.	2 1/2 tsp.
Flour equivalent	*2 1/3 cups*	*3 1/4 cups*	*4 1/3 cups*
Cycle	*whole wheat, sweet or basic cycle, timer*		
Setting	*medium*		

CREAM OF WHEAT BREAD

You'll have people wondering what your secret ingredient is. This slices extremely well and makes excellent French toast. Some people use the flavored packets of Cream of Wheat for variety.

	Small	**Medium**	**Large**
milk	1/2 cup	1 cup	1 1/4 cups
margarine or butter	2 tbs.	1/4 cup	5 tbs.
eggs	1	1	1
sugar	1 1/2 tbs.	2 tbs.	2 1/2 tbs.
salt	1/2 tsp.	3/4 tsp.	1 tsp.
bread flour	1 1/2 cups	2 cups	3 cups
Cream of Wheat, uncooked	2/3 cup	1 cup	1 1/3 cups
vital gluten, optional	1 tbs.	1 tbs.	1 1/2 tbs.
yeast	1 tsp.	1 1/2 tsp.	2 tsp.
Flour equivalent	*2+ cups*	*3 cups*	*4 1/3 cups*
Cycle	*whole wheat, sweet or basic cycle, no timer (eggs)*		
Setting	*medium*		

GRITS BREAD

This is just the thing for lovers of grits, Southern or not! The water is added while the machine is kneading to adjust the consistency. Leftover grits which have been refrigerated will be drier than freshly cooked grits.

	Small	**Medium**	**Large**
cooked grits	1 cup	1 1/2 cups	1 3/4 cups
margarine	1 tbs.	1 1/2 tbs.	2 tbs.
salt	3/4 tsp.	1 tsp.	1 tsp.
sugar	2 tsp.	1 tbs.	1 tbs.
bread flour	2 cups	2 1/4 cups	2 3/4 cups
yeast	1 tsp.	1 1/2 tsp.	2 tsp.
water	2–4 tbs.	1/3–1/2 cup	1/2–2/3 cup
Flour equivalent	*3 cups*	*3 3/4 cups*	*4 1/2 cups*
Cycle	*whole wheat, sweet or basic cycle, timer*		
Setting	*medium*		

KASHI BREAD

While usually found in the cereal section of a grocery store, kashi is actually a combination of the berries of seven grains. Several different cereals are sold by the same company — make sure you purchase the "breakfast pilaf" which requires cooking. Kashi may also be found in health food stores. Kashi requires approximately 30 minutes to cook in a water-to-grain ratio of 2:1. Adjust the dough with water if necessary.

	Small	**Medium**	**Large**
water	2/3 cup	3/4 cup	1 cup
margarine	1 tbs.	1 tbs.	1 1/2 tbs.
brown sugar	1 tbs.	1 1/2 tbs.	2 tbs.
salt	1/2 tsp.	3/4 tsp.	1 1/3 tsp.
cooked kashi	1/3 cup	1/2 cup	2/3 cup
whole wheat flour	1/3 cup	1/2 cup	2/3 cup
bread flour	1 3/4 cups	2 cups	2 2/3 cups
yeast	1 tsp.	1 1/2 tsp.	2 1/2 tsp.
Flour equivalent	*2 1/3 cups*	*3 cups*	*4 cups*
Cycle	*whole wheat, sweet or basic cycle, timer*		
Setting	*medium*		

NEW YORK RYE BREAD

This is a low-rising, dense, flavorful loaf. If you want a lighter loaf, add vital wheat gluten, available at health food stores. Caraway may be adjusted to taste. Serve this bread, dried, as bread crackers, with cheddar cheese and caraway seeds. Or, after the dough cycle, stuff with Gouda or sharp cheddar cheese cubes for appetizer pockets.

	Small	**Medium**	**Large**
water	7/8 cup	1 1/8 cups	1 1/3 cups
vegetable oil	1 tsp.	1 1/3 tbs.	1 1/2 tbs.
honey	1 1/2 tbs.	2 tbs.	2 1/2 tbs.
salt	3/4 tsp.	1 tsp.	1 tsp.
caraway seeds	2 tsp.	1 tbs.	1 tbs.
rye flour	1 cup	1 1/3 cups	1 1/2 cups
bread flour	1 3/4 cups	2 1/4 cups	2 2/3 cups
vital gluten, optional	2 tsp.	1 tbs.	1 1/2 tbs.
nonfat dry milk	3 tbs.	1/4 cup	1/3 cup
yeast	1 1/2 tsp.	2 1/2 tsp.	1 tbs.
Flour equivalent	*2 3/4 cups*	*3 1/2+ cups*	*4 1/2+ cups*
Cycle	*whole wheat, sweet or basic cycle, timer*		
Setting	*medium*		

SWEDISH RYE BREAD

The taste is a cross between rye and whole wheat with a slight flavor of orange. Very good. Caraway and orange zest may be adjusted to taste.

	Small	**Medium**	**Large**
water	7/8 cup	1 cup	1 1/4 cups
honey	2 tbs.	3 tbs.	1/4 cup
margarine or butter	1 tbs.	1 1/2 tbs.	2 tbs.
salt	3/4 tsp.	1 tsp.	1 tsp.
caraway seeds	2 tsp.	1 tbs.	1 1/2 tbs.
grated orange zest	1/2 tsp.	3/4 tsp.	1 tsp.
rye flour	1 cup	1 1/3 cups	1 1/2 cups
bread flour	1 1/2 cups	2 cups	2 1/2 cups
yeast	1 1/2 tsp.	2 tsp.	2 1/2 tsp.
Flour equivalent	*2 1/3 cups*	*3 1/2 cups*	*4 2/3 cups*
Cycle	*whole wheat, sweet or basic cycle, timer*		
Setting	*medium*		

NORWEGIAN RYE BREAD

This is my favorite rye. There is a large amount of flour in this recipe. If the dough seems dry or the machine sounds like it is struggling, add 1 to 2 tbs. water.

	Small	Medium	Large
water	3/4 cup	1 cup	1 1/4 cups
molasses	1/3 cup	1/3 cup	1/2 cup
margarine or butter	2 tbs.	2 1/2 tbs.	3 tbs.
salt	1/4 tsp.	1/2 tsp.	3/4 tsp.
caraway seeds	2 tsp.	1 tbs.	1 1/2 tbs.
whole wheat flour	1/4 cup	1/3 cup	1/2 cup
rye flour	1 1/4 cups	1 2/3 cups	2 1/2 cups
bread flour	1 1/4 cups	1 2/3 cups	2 1/2 cups
yeast	1 1/2 tsp.	2 tsp.	2 1/2 tsp.
Flour equivalent	*2 3/4 cups*	*3 2/3 cups*	*5 1/2 cups*
Cycle	*whole wheat, sweet or basic cycle, timer*		
Setting	*medium*		

LIGHT PUMPERNICKEL

This wonderful, light pumpernickel makes great sandwiches.

	Small	Medium	Large
water	2/3 cup	1 cup	1 1/3 cups
vegetable oil	1 1/2 tbs.	2 tbs.	3 tbs.
molasses	1 1/2 tbs.	2 tbs.	3 tbs.
sugar	2 tsp.	1 tbs.	1 1/2 tbs.
salt	1/2 tsp.	3/4 tsp.	1 tsp.
caraway seeds	1 1/2 tsp.	2 tsp.	1 tbs.
unsweetened cocoa	1 1/3 tbs.	2 tbs.	2 1/2 tbs.
rye flour	1 cup	1 1/2 cups	2 cups
bread flour	1 cup	1 1/2 cups	2 cups
vital gluten, optional	2 tsp.	1 tbs.	1 1/2 tbs.
yeast	1 tsp.	1 1/2 tsp.	2 1/2 tsp.
Flour equivalent	*2 cups*	*3 cups*	*4 cups*
Cycle	*whole wheat, sweet or basic cycle, timer*		
Setting	*medium*		

DARK PUMPERNICKEL

This is a heavy, dense bread which is terrific with soup and or or salad.

	Small	Medium	Large
water	1 cup	1 1/4 cups	1 1/2 cups
vegetable oil	2 tbs.	2 1/2 tbs.	3 tbs.
molasses	3 tbs.	1/4 cup	1/3 cup
unsweetened cocoa	1 1/2 tbs.	2 tbs.	2 1/2 tbs.
brown sugar	1 tbs.	1 1/2 tbs.	2 tbs.
instant coffee granules	1 tsp.	1 1/2 tsp.	2 tsp.
salt	3/4 tsp.	1 tsp.	1 1/2 tsp.
caraway seeds	2 tsp.	1 tbs.	1 tbs.
rye flour	3/4 cup	1 cup	1 1/4 cups
whole wheat flour	3/4 cup	1 cup	1 1/4 cups
bread flour	1 1/2 cups	2 cups	2 1/2 cups
yeast	1 1/2 tsp.	2 tsp.	2 1/2 tsp.
Flour equivalent	*3 cups*	*4 cups*	*5 cups*
Cycle	*whole wheat, sweet or basic cycle, timer*		
Setting	*medium*		

CORNMEAL BREAD

If you can find it, try blue cornmeal. This yeast cornmeal bread has a different texture than baking powder cornbread. Serve as bread crackers with cheese and jalapeño slices.

	Small	**Medium**	**Large**
water	3/4 cup	1 cup	1 1/3 cups
vegetable oil	1 tbs.	1 1/2 tbs.	2 tbs.
eggs	1	1	1
sugar	1 1/3 tbs.	2 tbs.	3 tbs.
salt	1/2 tsp.	1 tsp.	1 tsp.
yellow cornmeal	2/3 cup	1 cup	1 1/3 cups
bread flour	1 2/3 cups	2 cups	3 cups
yeast	1 tsp.	1 1/2 tsp.	2 1/2 tsp.
Flour equivalent	*2 1/3 cups*	*3 cups*	*4 1/3 cups*
Cycle	*whole wheat, sweet or basic cycle, no timer (eggs)*		
Setting	*medium*		

SPICY CORNMEAL: Add up to 2 tsp., 1 tbs., or 1 1/2 tbs. finely diced jalapeños or 1/2 tsp., 3/4 tsp. or 1 tsp. cayenne pepper.

HONEY CORNMEAL BREAD

This is a very tasty, slightly sweet cornmeal loaf. The dough may appear wet, but it should be high-rising and light in texture as a result.

	Small	Medium	Large
water	1/2 cup	3/4 cup	1 cup
vegetable oil	1 tbs.	1 1/2 tbs.	2 tbs.
honey	2 tbs.	3 tbs.	1/4 cup
eggs	2	3	4
salt	1/2 tsp.	1 tsp.	1 tsp.
cornmeal	2/3 cup	1 cup	1 1/3 cups
whole wheat flour	1/3 cup	1/2 cup	2/3 cup
bread flour	1 cup	1 1/2 cups	2 cups
yeast	1 tsp.	1 1/2 tsp.	2 1/2 tsp.
Flour equivalent	*2 cups*	*3 cups*	*4 cups*
Cycle	*whole wheat, sweet or basic cycle, no timer (eggs)*		
Setting	*medium*		

RICE BRAN BREAD

This is absolutely delicious. The rice bran and flour give this a slightly sweet taste. It is said that rice bran has the same cholesterol-lowering qualities as oat bran. If you can't find rice bran in your grocery store, look for it in health food stores.

	Small	**Medium**	**Large**
water	3/4 cup	1 cup	1 1/3 cups
margarine or butter	1 1/2 tbs.	2 tbs.	3 tbs.
sugar	2 tsp.	1 tbs.	1 1/2 tbs.
salt	3/4 tsp.	1 tsp.	1 tsp.
rice bran	1/3 cup	1/2 cup	2/3 cup
rice flour	1/3 cup	1/2 cup	2/3 cup
bread flour	1 1/2 cups	2 cups	3 cups
vital gluten, optional	2 tsp.	1 tbs.	1 tbs.
yeast	1 tsp.	1 1/2 tsp.	2 tsp.
Flour equivalent	*2+ cups*	*3 cups*	*4 1/3 cups*
Cycle	*whole wheat, sweet or basic cycle, timer*		
Setting	*medium*		

BARLEY BREAD

This is a delicious, light airy bread. Molasses may be used as a substitute for the barley malt syrup.

	Small	Medium	Large
water	3/4 cup	1 1/8 cups	1 1/3 cups
margarine or butter	1 tbs.	2 tbs.	2 1/2 tbs.
barley malt syrup	2 tbs.	3 tbs.	1/4 cup
sugar	3 tbs.	1/3 cup	1/3 cup
salt	1/2 tsp.	1 tsp.	1 tsp.
cinnamon	3/4 tsp.	1 tsp.	1 1/2 tsp.
barley flour	1/3 cup	1/2 cup	2/3 cup
bread flour	2 cups	3 cups	3 1/2 cups
yeast	1 tsp.	1 1/2 tsp.	2 1/2 tsp.
Flour equivalent	*2 1/3 cups*	*3 1/2 cups*	*4+ cups*
Cycle	*whole wheat, sweet or basic cycle, timer*		
Setting	*medium*		

BUCKWHEAT BREAD

This is a strong tasting bread — a must for buckwheat lovers.

	Small	**Medium**	**Large**
water	1 1/8 cups	1 1/4 cups	1 1/2 cups
vegetable oil	1 1/2 tbs.	2 tbs.	3 tbs.
honey	1 tbs.	1 1/2 tbs.	2 tbs.
salt	1/2 tsp.	1 tsp.	1 tsp.
buckwheat flour	1/2 cup	2/3 cup	3/4 cup
whole wheat flour	1 cup	1 1/3 cups	1 1/2 cups
bread flour	1 1/2 cups	2 cups	2 1/2 cups
yeast	1 1/2 tsp.	2 tsp.	2 tsp.
Flour equivalent	*2 1/2 cups*	*3 1/3 cups*	*4 cups*
Cycle	*whole wheat, sweet or basic cycle, timer*		
Setting	*medium*		

SOY FLAKES BREAD

The soy flakes give this bread a very unique texture and crunch. Kids love it. Soy flakes may be purchased at a health food store. I keep them on hand to add to homemade granola. Rye flakes may be substituted.

	Small	**Medium**	**Large**
water	2/3 cup	1 cup	1 1/3 cups
vegetable oil	1 1/2 tbs.	2 tbs.	3 tbs.
sugar	1 1/2 tbs.	2 tbs.	3 tbs.
salt	1/2 tsp.	3/4 tsp.	1 tsp.
soy flakes	1/3 cup	1/2 cup	2/3 cup
bread flour	1 3/4 cups	2 1/2 cups	3 cups
yeast	1 tsp.	1 1/2 tsp.	2 tsp.
Flour equivalent	*2+ cups*	*3 cups*	*3 2/3 cups*
Cycle	*whole wheat, sweet or basic cycle, timer*		
Setting	*medium*		

AMARANTH BREAD

Amaranth has a very unusual, distinct taste which is quite good and it is, of course, extremely nutritious. This is wonderful toasted.Find amaranth flour at health food stores and some large grocery stores.

	Small	**Medium**	**Large**
water	7/8 cup	1 cup	1 1/4 cups
margarine or butter	2 tbs.	3 tbs.	1/4 cup
sugar	2 tsp.	1 tbs.	1 1/2 tbs.
salt	1/2 tsp.	1 tsp.	1 tsp.
amaranth flour	1/3 cup	1/2 cup	2/3 cup
bread flour	2 cups	2 1/2 cups	3 1/2 cups
yeast	1 tsp.	1 1/2 tsp.	2 tsp.
Flour equivalent	*2 1/3 cups*	*3 cups*	*4+ cups*
Cycle	*whole wheat, sweet or basic cycle, timer*		
Setting	*medium*		

AMARANTH NUT BREAD

A wonderful nutty bread. Although it may be used for sandwiches, this is more of a dessert bread, I think. Use an egg white, yolk or 2 tbs. egg substitute for 1/2 egg.

	Small	**Medium**	**Large**
water	2/3 cup	1 cup	1 1/4 cups
vegetable oil	1 tbs.	2 tbs.	2 1/2 tbs.
honey	2 tbs.	3 tbs.	1/4 cup
egg	1/2	1	1
vanilla extract	1/2 tsp.	1 tsp.	1 tsp.
salt	1/2 tsp.	1 tsp.	1 1/2 tsp.
amaranth flour	1/3 cup	1/2 cup	2/3 cup
bread flour	1 3/4 cups	2 1/2 cups	3 1/3 cups
nonfat dry milk	2 tbs.	3 tbs.	1/4 cup
yeast	1 tsp.	1 1/2 tsp.	2 tsp.
At beep add: (If National or Panasonic, add following first kneading)			
chopped walnuts	1/3 cup	1/2 cup	2/3 cup
Flour equivalent	*2 1/2 cups*	*3 1/2 cups*	*4 2/3 cups*
Cycle	*whole wheat, sweet or basic cycle, no timer (eggs)*		
Setting	*medium*		

THREE-SEED BREAD

This bread has a wonderful taste and texture. Feel free to experiment with different seeds. Try combinations of anise, fennel, caraway or any other seeds you have on hand! This bread, along with the variation of Ancient Grain Bread, is great toasted or broiled with cheese.

	Small	**Medium**	**Large**
water	1 cup	1 1/2 cups	1 3/4 cups
vegetable oil	1 1/2 tbs.	2 tbs.	3 tbs.
honey	1 1/2 tsp.	2 tsp.	1 tbs.
salt	1/2 tsp.	3/4 tsp.	1 tsp.
sunflower seeds	3 tbs.	1/4 cup	1/3 cup
sesame seeds	1 1/2 tbs.	2 tbs.	3 tbs.
poppy seeds	1 tbs.	1 1/2 tbs.	2 tbs.
whole wheat flour	1 cup	1 1/3 cups	1 1/2 cups
bread flour	2 cups	2 3/4 cups	3 cups
nonfat dry milk	3 tbs.	1/4 cup	1/4 cup
yeast	1 tsp.	2 tsp.	2 1/2 tsp.
Flour equivalent	*3 cups*	*4+ cups*	*4 1/2 cups*
Cycle	*whole wheat, sweet or basic cycle, timer*		
Setting	*medium*		

ANCIENT GRAIN BREAD

This bread is a variation of Three-Seed Bread, *page 77. Great texture. A unique bread with the wonderful tastes of quinoa, amaranth, sesame seeds and poppy seeds. The quinoa and amaranth make this an extremely nutritious, healthy bread. In place of the seeds in* Three-Seed Bread, *substitute:*

	Small	**Medium**	**Large**
quinoa grains	1⅓ tbs.	2 tbs.	2⅔ tbs.
amaranth grains	1⅓ tbs.	2 tbs.	2⅔ tbs.
sesame seeds	2 tsp.	1 tbs.	1⅓ tbs.
poppy seeds	1¼ tsp.	2 tsp.	2½ tsp.

QUINOA BREAD

The quinoa gives this bread a nutty flavor. Great source of protein and calcium — worth trying. Ancient Harvest packages quinoa flour and it should be available through a good health food store.

	Small	**Medium**	**Large**
water	3/4 cup	1 1/8 cups	1 1/4 cups
margarine or butter	2 tbs.	1/4 cup	1/4 cup
sugar	1 1/2 tsp.	2 tsp.	1 tbs.
salt	1/2 tsp.	1 tsp.	1 1/2 tsp.
quinoa flour	1/3 cup	1/2 cup	3/4 cup
bread flour	2 cups	2 1/2 cups	3 cups
yeast	1 tsp.	1 1/2 tsp.	2 tsp.
Flour equivalent	*2 1/3 cups*	*3 cups*	*3 3/4 cups*
Cycle	*whole wheat, sweet or basic cycle, timer*		
Setting	*medium*		

SOURDOUGH BREADS

As the early day pioneers traveled west across the United States, they carried a mixture of flour and milk or water which was used to leaven bread. As the mixture or starter aged, it became more sour and, hence, so did the bread.

A true sourdough starter is nothing more than the flour and milk or water which sits at room temperature for several days and catches live yeast from the air. Most starter recipes today include yeast as an original starter ingredient as it is much easier and less time-consuming. In addition, many sourdough bread recipes also indicate usage of yeast itself as it does provide a higher rising, lighter loaf.

A sourdough starter should be kept in a glass or plastic bowl which has a tight-fitting lid. To make your starter, mix together: 2 cups lukewarm milk, 2 cups bread flour and 2½ tsp. (1 package) yeast.

I mix the starter with an electric hand-held mixer on the lowest setting. Cover your starter and place in a warm, draft-free location for 4 to 7 days, gently stirring it once a day. You may notice that the mixture bubbles and in some cases it may even overflow your bowl. This is an indication that you have a healthy fermenting process going on. A sour-smelling liquid may form on top of the starter which should simply be stirred back in.

If your starter ever changes colors, to purple, for example, discard and start another one.

After allowing your starter to sit for 4 to 7 days, it is ready to be used. Take out whatever portion your recipe calls for and put it into the machine as you would any liquid ingredient.

After removing a portion from the starter, the remaining starter must be "fed." Simply add equal portions of milk or water and flour as was used. For example, if you used 1 cup of starter, replace it with 1 cup of water and 1 cup of bread flour.

Some hints on feeding your starter: Always use the same kind of flour. If you used bread flour in your original starter, use bread flour to feed it. Also, alternate between milk and water for each feeding. Since your original liquid ingredient was milk, the first liquid feeding should be with water. If you forget which you used last, that's okay, but try to alternate at least every other time. After feeding your starter, let it sit at room temperature for approximately 1 day and then refrigerate. Many cookbooks suggest stirring the starter once a day even when being refrigerated; I find that it is not necessary.

You must, however, use a portion of the starter at least once a week. If you choose not to bake sourdough breads that often, then remove a cup of your starter and feed it as though you used some during the week. If this is not done, your starter will turn rancid and have to be replaced. Should you be away on vacation or otherwise unable to tend to the starter, freeze it. Upon your return, thaw it in the refrigerator and then remove a portion and feed it as soon as you are able.

My first few loaves of sourdough were not very sour and I feared it was my starter. After allowing the starter to mellow a little by sitting in the refrigerator and using only once a week, it and the breads became more sour.

Another hint is to put the ingredients on the timer cycle for early morning baking. The milk put in the night before adds a little more sour taste. If the bread is getting too sour for you, feed with water more often than milk.

Always check the consistency of the dough. The starter itself may vary from one day to the next and it is not uncommon to have to adjust the dough with water or flour.

If you use your starter frequently and/or it is very active and strong, it may be necessary to decrease the amount of yeast given in the recipe. This will require experimentation. It may even be possible to omit the yeast altogether if the bread is rising sufficiently with just the sourdough starter.

Many of the recipes in this chapter were adapted from ethnic recipes which called for a high amount of salt. If you feel the bread is too salty, you may safely cut the amount of salt to approximately 1 tsp. for a large size recipe.

SOURDOUGH BREAD

This compares favorably to the famous San Francisco sourdoughs. Adjust the consistency with the milk while the dough is kneading.

	Small	**Medium**	**Large**
starter	3/4 cup	1 cup	1 1/3 cups
margarine or butter	1 tbs.	2 tbs.	2 tbs.
sugar	1 1/2 tbs.	2 tbs.	2 1/2 tbs.
salt	1 tsp.	1 1/2 tsp.	1 1/2 tsp.
bread flour	2 cups	3 cups	3 1/2 cups
yeast	1 tsp.	1 1/2 tsp.	2 tsp.
milk	3 tbs.–1/3 cup	1/4–2/3 cup	1/4–3/4 cup
Flour equivalent	*2 1/3 cups*	*3 1/2 cups*	*4 1/4 cups*
Cycle	*basic, no timer (watch consistency)*		
Setting	*medium*		

SOURDOUGH WHEAT BREAD

A delicious sourdough with the benefits of whole wheat flour. Adjust the consistency with the milk while the dough is kneading.

	Small	Medium	Large
starter	7/8 cup	1 cup	1 1/2 cups
margarine or butter	1 tbs.	2 tbs.	2 1/2 tbs.
sugar	1 1/2 tbs.	2 tbs.	2 1/2 tbs.
salt	1 tsp.	1 1/2 tsp.	1 1/2 tsp.
whole wheat flour	3/4 cup	1 cup	1 1/2 cups
bread flour	1 1/2 cups	2 cups	2 1/2 cups
yeast	1 tsp.	2 tsp.	2 tsp.
milk	3 tbs.–1/3 cup	1/4–2/3 cup	1/2–3/4 cup
Flour equivalent	*2 1/3 cups*	*3 1/2 cups*	*4 3/4 cups*
Cycle	*basic, no timer (watch consistency)*		
Setting	*medium*		

SOURDOUGH FRENCH BREAD

This is absolutely delicious — great for sandwiches. Adjust the consistency with the water while the dough is kneading.

	Small	**Medium**	**Large**
starter	2/3 cup	1 cup	1 1/3 cups
sugar	1 tsp.	1 1/2 tsp.	2 tsp.
salt	1/2 tsp.	3/4 tsp.	1 tsp.
bread flour	2 cups	3 cups	4 cups
yeast	1 tsp.	1 1/2 tsp.	2 tsp.
water	1/4–1/3 cup	1/2–2/3 cup	2/3–3/4 cup
Flour equivalent	*2 1/3 cups*	*3 1/2 cups*	*4 2/3 cups*
Cycle	*basic, no timer (watch consistency)*		
Setting	*medium*		

SOURDOUGH PIZZA CRUST

This is an interesting change of pace in pizza making. The small recipe makes one thin 15″ crust, the medium recipe makes two thin 10″ crusts and the large recipe makes two thin 15″ crusts. Any size can be made in your machine because it is not being baked. Add 1 tbs. water at a time as needed to adjust the consistency of the dough.

	Small	**Medium**	**Large**
starter	1/2 cup	3/4 cup	1 cup
olive oil	1 1/2 tbs.	2 1/4 tbs.	3 tbs.
salt	1/2 tsp.	3/4 tsp.	1 tsp.
all-purpose flour	2 cups	3 cups	4 cups
yeast	1 tsp.	1 1/2 tsp.	2 tsp.
water	as needed	as needed	as needed

Remove dough from the machine upon completion of the dough cycle. Roll on a lightly floured surface into a rectangle or circle, depending on the pan to be used. Brush very lightly with additional olive oil. If you want a thicker crust, cover dough and let rise for about 30 minutes. Heat oven to 500°. If you want a thin crust, top with pizza sauce and desired toppings and bake immediately until crust is brown and cheese is melted, 5 to 10 minutes.

SOURDOUGH CORNMEAL BREAD

This one is a unique, delicious bread. Adjust the consistency with the milk while the dough is kneading.

	Small	**Medium**	**Large**
starter	2/3 cup	1 cup	1 1/3 cups
margarine or butter	1 tbs.	1 1/2 tbs.	2 tbs.
sugar	1 tbs.	1 1/2 tbs.	2 tbs.
salt	1/2 tsp.	3/4 tsp.	1 tsp.
cornmeal	2/3 cup	1 cup	1 1/3 cups
bread flour	1 1/2 cups	2 1/2 cups	2 2/3 cups
yeast	1 tsp.	1 1/2 tsp.	2 1/2 tsp.
milk	2–4 tbs.	1/4–1/3 cup	1/3–1/2 cup
Flour equivalent	*3 cups*	*4 cups*	*4 2/3 cups*
Cycle	*basic, no timer (watch consistency)*		
Setting	*medium*		

SOURDOUGH RYE BREAD

This slightly sour loaf is very light. It is different from many sourdoughs as it has its own starter, which is used in its entirety in the recipe. Molasses may be substituted for barley malt syrup.

	Small	Medium	Large
Starter*			
warm milk (115º)	1/2 cup	3/4 cup	1 cup
rye flour	1/2 cup	3/4 cup	1 cup
yeast	1 tsp.	1 tsp.	1 1/2 tsp.

To prepare starter: Sprinkle yeast over warm milk and stir until dissolved; stir in rye flour. Cover and let stand at room temperature for 3 days, stirring once a day. Use the entire starter in your bread recipe on the next page.

	Small	Medium	Large
Rye Starter	*	*	*
water	1/3 cup	1/2 cup	2/3 cup
egg	1/2	1	1
vegetable oil	1 tbs.	1 1/2 tbs.	2 tbs.
barley malt syrup	1 tbs.	1 1/2 tbs.	2 tbs.
salt	1 tsp.	1 1/2 tsp.	2 tsp.
caraway seeds	2 tsp.	1 tbs.	1 1/3 tbs.
bread flour	1 3/4 cups	2 1/2 cups	3 cups
rye flour	1/2 cup	3/4 cup	1 cup
yeast	1 tsp.	1 1/2 tsp.	2 1/2 tsp.
Flour equivalent	*2 3/4 cups*	*4 cups*	*5 cups*
Cycle	*basic, no timer (watch consistency)*		
Setting	*medium*		

SOURDOUGH OATMEAL BREAD

This is a very moist sourdough bread. Adjust the consistency with the milk while the dough is kneading.

	Small	Medium	Large
Starter	3/4 cup	1 cup	1 1/4 cups
margarine or butter	1 tbs.	1 1/2 tbs.	2 tbs.
sugar	1 tbs.	1 1/2 tbs.	2 tbs.
salt	3/4 tsp.	1 tsp.	1 tsp.
rolled oats	3/4 cup	1 cup	1 1/4 cups
bread flour	2 1/4 cups	3 cups	3 1/2 cups
yeast	1 1/2 tsp.	2 tsp.	2 tsp.
milk	1/3–1/2 cup	1/2–2/3 cup	2/3–3/4 cup
Flour equivalent	*3 1/3 cups*	*4 1/2 cups*	*5 1/2 cups*
Cycle	*basic, no timer (watch consistency)*		
Setting	*medium*		

FRUIT AND VEGETABLE BREADS

Fruits and vegetables, sometimes used as the main liquid ingredient in recipes, may vary in their liquid content. Check dough after 5 to 10 minutes of kneading and add water or flour if necessary.

APPLE BUTTER BREAD

Bake the apple butter right into the bread. Try substituting any favorite jam or jelly for the apple butter. This is a high-rising bread. If in doubt, make a smaller size.

	Small	**Medium**	**Large**
water	3/4 cup	1 cup	1 1/3 cups
vegetable oil	1 1/2 tbs.	2 tbs.	3 tbs.
apple butter	1/3 cup	1/2 cup	2/3 cup
sugar	2 tsp.	1 tbs.	1 1/2 tbs.
salt	3/4 tsp.	1 tsp.	1 tsp.
whole wheat flour	2/3 cup	1 cup	1 1/3 cups
bread flour	1 1/2 cups	2 cups	2 3/4 cups
yeast	1 tsp.	1 1/2 tsp.	2 tsp.
Flour equivalent	*2+ cups*	*3 cups*	*3 3/4 cups*
Cycle	*sweet, basic, timer*		
Setting	*light to medium*		

APPLE CHUNK BREAD

You'll think you're eating an apple pie. The apples add moisture to the dough. Add the apples at the beginning of the second kneading cycle. If your machine has only one main kneading cycle, add apples at the beginning. Add 1 to 2 tbs. of flour to adjust consistency if necessary. This dessert bread should be served warm (it probably won't last long enough to get cold anyway).

	Small	**Medium**	**Large**
milk	2/3 cup	1 cup	1 1/4 cups
vegetable oil	2 tbs.	3 tbs.	3 tbs.
sugar	1 1/2 tbs.	2 tbs.	2 1/2 tbs.
cinnamon	1/2 tsp.	1/2 tsp.	1 tsp.
salt	1 tsp.	1 1/2 tsp.	1 1/2 tsp.
bread flour	2 cups	3 cups	3 1/2 cups
yeast	1 tsp.	1 1/2 tsp.	2 tsp.
medium apple, peeled and diced	1/2	1 1/2	1 1/2
Flour equivalent	*2 cups*	*3 cups*	*4 cups*
Cycle	*sweet, basic, no timer (watch consistency)*		
Setting	*light to medium*		

APPLESAUCE BREAD

This bread made a huge hit at a neighborhood potluck — the children especially kept going back for more. Very moist. The applesauce is the main source of liquid – watch the consistency and add water or flour as necessary.

	Small	**Medium**	**Large**
applesauce	1 cup	1¼ cups	1¾ cups
margarine or butter	2 tbs.	2 tbs.	3 tbs.
sugar	1 tbs.	1½ tbs.	2 tbs.
salt	1 tsp.	1 tsp.	1½ tsp.
cinnamon, optional	1 tsp.	1 tsp.	1½ tsp.
whole wheat flour	¾ cup	1 cup	1¼ cups
bread flour	1½ cups	2 cups	2½ cups
yeast	1½ tsp.	2 tsp.	2½ tsp.
Flour equivalent	*2¼ cups*	*3 cups*	*3¾ cups*
Cycle	*sweet, basic, no timer (watch consistency)*		
Setting	*light to medium*		

BANANA OATMEAL BREAD

This low-rising bread has a slight taste of banana with the "feel" of oatmeal. The flavor of the banana seems to be stronger when the bread is toasted. Use fully ripe bananas and adjust the dough consistency with the extra water if you need to.

	Small	**Medium**	**Large**
water	1/3–1/2 cup	1/2–2/3 cup	1/2–3/4 cup
mashed banana	3/4 cup	1 cup	1 1/4 cups
vegetable oil	2 tbs.	2 1/2 tbs.	3 tbs.
sugar	1 tbs.	1 1/2 tbs.	2 tbs.
salt	1 tsp.	1 tsp.	1 1/2 tsp.
rolled oats	1 cup	1 1/3 cups	1 3/4 cups
bread flour	2 cups	2 2/3 cups	3 cups
yeast	1 1/2 tsp.	2 tsp.	2 1/2 tsp.
Flour equivalent	*3 cups*	*4 cups*	*4 3/4 cups*
Cycle	*sweet, basic, no timer (watch consistency)*		
Setting	*light to medium*		

BLUEBERRY BREAD

Delicious — try blue cornmeal although yellow will do nicely too. If using frozen blueberries, they must be well thawed and tightly packed into your measuring cup. Adjust the consistency with the water as the dough is kneading. This low-rising, dense bread is full of flavor This is wonderful toasted with cream cheese or as French toast with a blueberry syrup.

	Small	**Medium**	**Large**
cottage cheese	1/2 cup	2/3 cup	3/4 cup
margarine or butter	1 1/2 tbs.	2 tbs.	2 tbs.
blueberries	3/4 cup	1 cup	1 1/4 cups
sugar	2 tbs.	2 1/2 tbs.	3 tbs.
salt	1 tsp.	1 1/2 tsp.	1 1/2 tsp.
blue cornmeal	1 cup	1 1/3 cups	1 1/2 cups
bread flour	2 cups	2 2/3 cups	3 cups
yeast	1 1/2 tsp.	2 tsp.	2 1/2 tsp.
water	2–4 tbs.	3 tbs.–1/3 cup	1/4–1/2 cup
Flour equivalent	*3 cups*	*4 cups*	*4 1/2 cups*
Cycle	*sweet, basic, no timer (watch consistency)*		
Setting	*light to medium*		

CARROT BREAD

This delicious, healthy bread is a good way to get your beta carotene! Much of the liquid comes from the grated carrot – watch the consistency and add water or flour if necessary. There is a high amount of low-rising flour, *see page 22.*

	Small	**Medium**	**Large**
water	3/4 cup	7/8 cup	1 1/4 cups
vegetable oil	1 tbs.	1 1/2 tbs.	2 tbs.
grated carrot	1/2 cup	2/3 cup	3/4 cup
brown sugar	1 1/2 tbs.	2 tbs.	2 1/2 tbs.
salt	1 tsp.	1 tsp.	1 1/2 tsp.
rolled oats	1 cup	1 1/3 cups	1 1/2 cups
whole wheat flour	1/2 cup	2/3 cup	3/4 cup
bread flour	1 1/2 cups	2 cups	2 1/2 cups
nonfat dry milk	3 tbs.	1/4 cup	1/3 cup
yeast	1 tsp.	1 1/2 tsp.	2 tsp.
Flour equivalent	*3 cups*	*4 cups*	*4 3/4 cups*
Cycle	*sweet, basic, no timer (watch consistency)*		
Setting	*light to medium*		

COCONUT PINEAPPLE BREAD

Wonderful. A must for Sunday brunch or dessert. Fun for a "Hawaiian luau" dinner. Adjust the consistency of the dough with the water as the dough is kneading. This makes fabulous French toast.

	Small	**Medium**	**Large**
cream cheese	4 oz	6 oz	8 oz.
can (8 oz.) crushed pineapple, drained	1/2 can	1 can	1 can
pineapple extract	1 tsp.	1 1/2 tsp.	2 tsp.
vegetable oil	2 tbs.	3 tbs.	3 tbs.
sugar	2 tbs.	3 tbs.	3 tbs.
salt	3/4 tsp.	1 tsp.	1 tsp.
sweetened grated coconut	3 tbs.	1/4 cup	1/3 cup
bread flour	2 cups	3 cups	3 1/2 cups
yeast	1 tsp.	1 1/2 tsp.	2 tsp.
water	1–3 tbs.	2–4 tbs.	1/4–1/3 cup
Flour equivalent	*2 cups*	*3 cups*	*3 1/2 cups*
Cycle	*sweet, basic, no timer (watch consistency)*		
Setting	*light to medium*		

LEMON BREAD

This lightly colored bread has a subtle, pleasing flavor. The lemon zest may be adjusted to taste. Serve as a side to a fish or chicken dinner.

	Small	**Medium**	**Large**
water	2/3 cup	1 cup	1 1/4 cups
margarine or butter	1 tbs.	2 tbs.	2 tbs.
grated lemon zest	3/4 tsp.	1 tsp.	1 1/2 tsp.
sugar	1/2 tsp.	3/4 tsp.	1 tsp.
salt	1/4 tsp.	1/2 tsp.	3/4 tsp.
bread flour	2 cups	3 cups	3 1/2 cups
nonfat dry milk	2 tbs.	1/4 cup	1/3 cup
yeast	1 tsp.	1 1/2 tsp.	2 tsp.
Flour equivalent	*3 cups*	*4 cups*	*4 3/4 cups*
Cycle	*sweet, basic; timer*		
Setting	*medium*		

ONION BREAD

Even if you typically do not like onions, you'll like this bread. It is a great accompaniment to barbecue dinners — chicken or burgers. Onions vary in moisture content, so you may have to adjust the consistency. For a real treat on a cold rainy or snowy day, make the dough from this recipe into Bread Bowls *for bean soup,* *see page 26.* *Or, use the dough and make appetizer pockets with sharp cheddar cheese. Use the bread for grilled cheese, leftovers for croutons, or bread crackers.*

	Small	**Medium**	**Large**
water	1/2 cup	3/4 cup	1 cup
margarine or butter	1 tbs.	1 1/2 tbs.	2 tbs.
grated fresh onion	1/3 cup	1/2 cup	2/3 cup
sugar	2 tsp.	1 tbs.	1 1/2 tbs.
salt	3/4 tsp.	1 tsp.	1 1/2 tsp.
whole wheat flour	1/3 cup	1/2 cup	2/3 cup
bread flour	1 3/4 cups	2 1/2 cups	3 1/3 cups
yeast	1 tsp.	1 1/2 tsp.	2 1/2 tsp.
Flour equivalent	*2+ cups*	*3 cups*	*4 cups*
Cycle	*basic, no timer (watch consistency)*		
Setting	*medium*		

ORANGE BANANA BREAD

This unique breakfast bread is just as good toasted as fresh out of the oven. Use very ripe bananas and adjust the consistency with additional orange juice if necessary. This makes fabulous French toast.

	Small	Medium	Large
orange juice	1/2 cup	3/4 cup	7/8 cup
margarine or butter	1/2 tbs.	1 tbs.	1 tbs.
mashed banana	1/3 cup	1/2 cup	2/3 cup
sugar	2 tsp.	1 tbs.	1 1/2 tbs.
grated orange zest	1/2 tsp.	3/4 tsp.	1 tsp.
salt	1/2 tsp.	3/4 tsp.	1 tsp.
bread flour	2 cups	3 cups	3 1/2 cups
yeast	1 1/2 tsp.	2 tsp.	2 tsp.
Flour equivalent	*2 cups*	*3 cups*	*3 1/2 cups*
Cycle	*sweet, basic, no timer (watch consistency)*		
Setting	*light to medium*		

ORANGE CINNAMON BREAD

Set it on the timer cycle and wake up to it hot from the oven, or have it toasted the next day, if it lasts that long. Both the cinnamon and the orange zest may be adjusted to taste. This makes wonderful French toast or regular toast with sweetened butter andpreserves.

	Small	**Medium**	**Large**
orange juice	3/4 cup	1 1/8 cups	1 1/3 cups
margarine or butter	1 tbs.	2 tbs.	2 tbs.
cinnamon	1 tsp.	2 tsp.	1 tbs.
grated orange zest	3/4 tsp.	1 tsp.	1 tsp.
salt	1/2 tsp.	3/4 tsp.	1 tsp.
sugar	1 tsp.	2 tsp.	1 tbs.
bread flour	2 cups	3 cups	3 1/2 cups
yeast	1 1/2 tsp.	2 tsp.	2 1/2 tsp.
Flour equivalent	*2 cups*	*3 cups*	*3 1/2 cups*
Cycle	*sweet, basic, no timer (watch consistency)*		
Setting	*light to medium*		

ORANGE CRAISIN BREAD: add 1/4 cup, 1/2 cup or 3/4 cup Craisins. You may use or omit the cinnamon.

PEANUT BUTTER AND JELLY BREAD

Kids love this bread! Watch this dough carefully and add water or scrape the sides of the pan if necessary. Jam seems to have too high a sugar content, so make sure to use a jelly. This is a high-rising loaf. If in doubt about the size, use the next smaller recipe. Glass-domed machines should make the medium size for best results. The whole wheat flour (and nutrition!) is hidden from the kids – it's the peanut butter that makes the bread dark in color!

	Small	**Medium**	**Large**
water	2/3 cup	1 cup	1 1/3 cups
vegetable oil	1 tbs.	1 1/2 tbs.	2 tbs.
peanut butter	1/3 cup	1/2 cup	2/3 cup
jelly	1/3 cup	1/2 cup	2/3 cup
sugar	2 tsp.	1 tbs.	1 1/3 tbs.
salt	2/3 tsp.	1 tsp.	1 tsp.
whole wheat flour	2/3 cup	1 cup	1 1/3 cups
bread flour	1 1/3 cups	2 cups	2 2/3 cups
yeast	1 tsp.	1 1/2 tsp.	2 1/2 tsp.
Flour equivalent	*2 cups*	*3 cups*	*4 cups*
Cycle	*sweet, basic, no timer (watch consistency)*		
Setting	*light to medium*		

POPPY SEED BREAD

Expect a high-rising loaf when you make this very light, airy bread. Eat it alone or try it topped with hot ham and cheese. This makes fabulous French toast.

	Small	**Medium**	**Large**
water	2/3 cup	1 cup	1 1/4 cups
vegetable oil	1 tbs.	1 1/2 tbs.	2 tbs.
vanilla extract	1/2 tsp.	1 tsp.	1 tsp.
butter flavoring	1/2 tsp.	1 tsp.	1 tsp.
almond extract	1/2 tsp.	1 tsp.	1 tsp.
salt	3/4 tsp.	1 tsp.	1 tsp.
sugar	2 tbs.	3 tbs.	1/4 cup
poppy seeds	1 1/2 tbs.	2 tbs.	3 tbs.
bread flour	2 cups	3 cups	3 1/2 cups
yeast	1 tsp.	1 1/2 tsp.	2 tsp.
Flour equivalent	*2 cups*	*3 cups*	*3 1/2 cups*
Cycle	*sweet, basic, timer*		
Setting	*light to medium*		

POTATO BREAD

This potato bread is really good alone or as sandwich bread. The potatoes give it just a little extra flavor. This is high-rising. If in doubt about the size, use a smaller size. This bread slices very well. Use an egg yolk, white or 2 tbs. egg substitute for the 1/2 egg. A few hours before making the bread, boil 1 to 2 peeled potatoes. Save water to use in bread. Mash potatoes, without milk or butter, and let cool to lukewarm or room temperature.

	Small	**Medium**	**Large**
potato water	1/2 cup	2/3 cup	3/4 cup
margarine or butter	2 tbs.	2 1/2 tbs.	3 tbs.
egg	1/2	1/2	1
mashed potatoes	1/3 cup	1/3 cup	1/2 cup
sugar	1 1/2 tbs.	2 tbs.	2 tbs.
salt	3/4 tsp.	1 tsp.	1 tsp.
bread flour	2 cups	2 1/2 cups	3 cups
yeast	1 tsp.	1 1/2 tsp.	2 tsp.
Flour equivalent	*2 cups*	*2 1/2 cups*	*3 cups*
Cycle	*sweet, basic, no timer (watch consistency)*		
Setting	*light to medium*		

RAISIN BREAD

A friend of mine tasted this bread and went out the next day to buy an automatic bread machine. Need I say more? Craisins (dried, sweetened cranberries) are now readily available in virtually all grocery stores and come in a variety of flavors. Try substituting Craisins for raisins for a little variety. Any of these variations make fabulous French toast.

	Small	**Medium**	**Large**
water	3/4 cup	1 1/8 cups	1 1/4 cups
margarine or butter	1 1/2 tbs.	2 tbs.	2 tbs.
sugar	1 1/2 tbs.	2 tbs.	2 1/2 tbs.
salt	3/4 tsp.	1 tsp.	1 tsp.
bread flour	2 cups	3 cups	3 1/2 cups
yeast	1 tsp.	1 1/2 tsp.	2 tsp.
At beep add: (If National or Panasonic, add following first kneading)			
raisins	1/2 cup	3/4 cup	1 cup
Flour equivalent	*2 cups*	*3 cups*	*3 1/2 cups*
Cycle	*sweet, basic, no timer (add raisins at beep)*		
Setting	*light to medium*		

VARIATIONS

All the following ingredients are put in the machine when it beeps (or during the rest period after the first kneading in National or Panasonic machines).

	Small	Medium	Large
CINNAMON RAISIN BREAD			
raisins	1/2 cup	3/4 cup	1 cup
cinnamon	2 tsp.	1 tbs.	1 tbs.
APRICOT BREAD			
dried apricots, chopped	1/2 cup	3/4 cup	1 cup
MIXED DRIED FRUIT BREAD			
mixed dried fruit, chopped	1/2 cup	3/4 cup	1 cup
ORANGE RAISIN BREAD			
raisins	1/2 cup	3/4 cup	1 cup
grated orange zest	1/3 tsp.	1/2 tsp.	1 tsp.

PISTACHIO RAISIN BREAD

You won't believe how good this one is. While any nut could be used, the pistachio seems to have that right flavor!

	Small	Medium	Large
water	2/3 cup	1 cup	1 1/3 cups
vegetable oil	1 tbs.	1 1/2 tbs.	2 tbs.
honey	1 tbs.	1 1/2 tbs.	2 tbs.
salt	1/2 tsp.	1 tsp.	1tsp.
whole wheat flour	1/2 cup	3/4 cup	1 cup
bread flour	1 1/2 cups	2 1/4 cups	3 cups
yeast	1 tsp.	1 1/2 tsp.	2 tsp.
At beep add: (If National or Panasonic, add following first kneading)			
raisins	2 tbs.	3 tbs.	1/4 cup
pistachio nuts	2 tbs.	3 tbs.	1/4 cup

Flour equivalent	*2 cups*	*3 cups*	*3 1/2 cups*
Cycle	*sweet, basic, no timer (add raisins/pistachios at beep)*		
Setting	*light to medium*		

PUMPKIN/WINTER SQUASH BREAD

This bread is great way to hide vegetables from finicky eaters. Use cooked, mashed acorn, butternut or hubbard squash or even canned pumpkin in this recipe. Watch the consistency.

	Small	Medium	Large
water	1/2 cup	3/4 cup	1 cup
winter squash, cooked and mashed	1/3 cup	2/3 cup	3/4 cup
vegetable oil	1 1/2 tbs.	2 tbs.	3 tbs.
honey	1 1/2 tbs.	2 tbs.	3 tbs.
salt	1 tsp.	1 1/2 tsp.	2 tsp.
cinnamon	3/4 tsp.	1 tsp.	1 1/3 tsp.
ground allspice	1/4 tsp.	1/2 tsp.	3/4 tsp.
nutmeg	1/8 tsp.	1/4 tsp.	1/2 tsp.
ground cloves	1/8 tsp.	1/4 tsp.	1/2 tsp.
whole wheat flour	1/3 cup	1/2 cup	2/3 cup
bread flour	1 2/3 cups	2 1/2 cups	3 1/3 cups
yeast	1 tsp.	1 1/2 tsp.	2 1/2 tsp.
Flour equivalent	*2 cups*	*3 cups*	*4 cups*
Cycle	*sweet, basic, no timer (watch consistency)*		
Setting	*light to medium*		

IRISH SODA BREAD

While at first you may wonder about the caraway seed and raisin combination, once you've tried it, you'll be hooked.

	Small	**Medium**	**Large**
buttermilk	3/4 cup	1 1/8 cups	1 1/3 cups
margarine or butter	1 1/2 tbs.	2 tbs.	3 tbs.
sugar	1 1/2 tbs.	2 tbs.	2 1/2 tbs.
salt	3/4 tsp.	1 tsp.	1 tsp.
baking soda	1/4 tsp.	1/2 tsp.	1/2 tsp.
caraway seeds	1 1/2 tsp.	2 tsp.	1 tbs.
bread flour	2 cups	3 cups	3 1/2 cups
yeast	1 1/2 tsp.	2 tsp.	2 1/2 tsp.
At beep add: (If National or Panasonic, add following first kneading)			
raisins	1/4 cup	1/3 cup	1/2 cup
Flour equivalent	*2 cups*	*3 cups*	*3 1/2 cups*
Cycle	*sweet, basic, no timer (add raisins at beep)*		
Setting	*light to medium*		

SUNFLOWER BREAD

The sunflower seeds make an interesting change from a raisin bread. Terrific flavor. Try substituting pumpkin seeds for another interesting, tasty variation.

	Small	Medium	Large
water	2/3 cup	1 cup	1 1/3 cups
vegetable oil	1 tbs.	1 1/2 tbs.	2 tbs.
honey	1 1/2 tbs.	2 tbs.	2 1/2 tbs.
salt	1/2 tsp.	3/4 tsp.	1 tsp.
rolled oats	1/3 cup	1/2 cup	2/3 cup
whole wheat flour	1/3 cup	1/2 cup	2/3 cup
bread flour	1 1/2 cups	2 cups	2 2/3 cups
yeast	1 tsp.	1 1/2 tsp.	2 tsp.
At beep add: (If National or Panasonic, add following first kneading)			
sunflower seeds	1/3 cup	1/2 cup	2/3 cup
raisins	1/4 cup	1/4 cup	1/3 cup
Flour equivalent	*2+ cups*	*3 cups*	*4 cups*
Cycle	*sweet, basic, no timer (add sunflower seeds/raisins at beep)*		
Setting	*light to medium*		

STOLLEN

If this bread does not bake properly, reduce the amount of fruits.

	Small	Medium	Large
milk	1/2–2/3 cup	2/3–3/4 cup	7/8–1 cup
margarine or butter	2 tbs.	3 tbs.	1/4 cup
egg	1	1	1
almond extract	1/4 tsp.	1/4 tsp.	1/2 tsp.
rum extract	1/4 tsp.	1/4 tsp.	1/2 tsp.
sugar	2 tbs.	3 tbs.	1/4 cup
salt	3/4 tsp.	1 tsp.	1 tsp.
mace	1/8 tsp.	1/8 tsp.	1/4 tsp.
cardamom	pinch	pinch	1/8 tsp.
grated lemon zest	1 1/2 tsp.	2 tsp.	1 tbs.
grated orange zest	1 1/2 tsp.	2 tsp.	1 tbs.
bread flour	2 cups	3 cups	3 1/2 cups
yeast	1 tsp.	1 1/2 tsp.	2 tsp.
At the beep add: (If National or Panasonic, add following first kneading)			
slivered almonds	1/4 cup	1/3 cup	1/2 cup
mixed dried fruit, chopped	1/4 cup	1/3 cup	1/2 cup

PANETTONE

Candied fruit is traditionally used in panettone recipes, but some machines have difficulty baking the high sugar content. Try dried mixed fruits instead. Glass-domed machines should make the medium size. This is perfect for French toast.

	Small	**Medium**	**Large**
water	1/2 cup	2/3 cup	3/4 cup
margarine or butter	3 tbs.	1/4 cup	5 tbs.
eggs	1	1 1/2	1 1/2
sugar	3 tbs.	1/4 cup	1/3 cup
salt	1/2 tsp.	3/4 tsp.	1 tsp.
grated lemon zest	1 tsp.	1 1/2 tsp.	1 1/2 tsp.
bread flour	2 cups	3 cups	3 1/2 cups
yeast	1 tsp.	1 1/2 tsp.	2 tsp.
At beep add: (If National or Panasonic, add following first kneading)			
mixed dried fruits, chopped	2 tbs.	3 tbs.	1/4 cup
chopped nuts	2 tbs.	3 tbs.	1/4 cup
Flour equivalent	*2 cups*	*3 cups*	*3 1/2 cups*
Cycle	*sweet, basic, no timer (add fruit/nuts at beep)*		
Setting	*light to medium*		

SALSA CORNMEAL BREAD

This wonderful cornmeal bread has just a hint of hot and spicy salsa. Serve this low-rising bread with any Mexican meal. Adjust the consistency of the dough if necessary.

	Small	**Medium**	**Large**
milk	2/3 cup	7/8 cup	1 cup
salsa	2 tbs.	3 tbs.	1/4 cup
margarine or butter	1 1/2 tbs.	2 tbs.	2 1/2 tbs.
egg	1	1	1
sugar	2 tsp.	1 tbs.	1 1/2 tbs.
salt	3/4 tsp.	1 tsp.	1 1/2 tsp.
yellow cornmeal	2/3 cup	1 cup	1 1/3 cups
bread flour	2 cups	2 1/2 cups	3 cups
yeast	1 tsp.	1 1/2 tsp.	2 tsp.
Flour equivalent	*2 2/3 cups*	*3 1/2 cups*	*4 1/3 cups*
Cycle	*basic, no timer (watch consistency)*		
Setting	*medium*		

STRAWBERRY BANANA BREAD

This wonderful, light loaf has just the right hint of both strawberries and banana. Use ripe bananas and adjust the consistency with additional milk or flour if necessary. This makes a lovely French toast.

	Small	**Medium**	**Large**
milk	1/4 cup	1/3 cup	1/2 cup
mashed strawberries	1/4 cup	1/3 cup	1/2 cup
mashed bananas	1/4 cup	1/3 cup	1/2 cup
margarine	1 tbs.	1 1/2 tbs.	2 tbs.
sugar	1 tsp.	1 1/2 tsp.	2 tsp.
salt	1/2 tsp.	3/4 tsp.	1 tsp.
bread flour	2 cups	2 1/2 cups	3 1/2 cups
yeast	1 tsp.	1 1/2 tsp.	2 1/2 tsp.
Flour equivalent	*2 cups*	*2 1/2 cups*	*3 1/2 cups*
Cycle	*sweet, basic, no timer (watch consistency)*		
Setting	*light to medium*		

SWEET POTATO BREAD

Just a hint of sweet potatoes makes this a perfect accompaniment to a turkey dinner and is great later for the leftover sandwiches. Cinnamon or nutmeg may be adjusted to taste if desired. Peel and boil a large sweet potato, then mash plain — no milk or butter. Save the cooking water for the first ingredient!

	Small	**Medium**	**Large**
sweet potato water	1/2 cup	3/4 cup	7/8 cup
mashed sweet potatoes	1/3 cup	1/2 cup	2/3 cup
margarine or butter	2 tbs.	3 tbs.	3 tbs.
brown sugar	2 tbs.	3 tbs.	1/4 cup
salt	3/4 tsp.	1 tsp.	1 1/2 tsp.
cinnamon or nutmeg	1/2 tsp.	3/4 tsp.	1 tsp.
bread flour	2 cups	3 cups	3 1/2 cups
yeast	1 tsp.	1 1/2 tsp.	2 tsp.
Flour equivalent	*2 cups*	*2 1/2 cups*	*3 1/2 cups*
Cycle	*sweet, basic, no timer (watch consistency)*		
Setting	*light to medium*		

ZUCCHINI WHEAT BREAD

Zucchini lovers will be especially happy with this one. Toasting brings out a stronger flavor. Watch the consistency and adjust with water or flour as needed.

	Small	**Medium**	**Large**
shredded zucchini	1/2 cup	3/4 cup	1 cup
water	1/2 cup	3/4 cup	1 cup
vegetable oil	2 tbs.	3 tbs.	1/4 cup
honey	2 tbs.	3 tbs.	1/4 cup
salt	1/2 tsp.	3/4 tsp.	1 tsp.
grated orange zest	3/4 tsp.	1 tsp.	1 1/2 tsp.
wheat germ	3 tbs.	1/4 cup	1/3 cup
whole wheat flour	1 cup	1 1/2 cups	2 cups
bread flour	1 cup	1 1/2 cups	2 cups
yeast	1 tsp.	1 1/2 tsp.	2 tsp.
Flour equivalent	*2 cups*	*3 cups*	*4 cups*
Cycle	*sweet, basic, no timer (watch consistency)*		
Setting	*light to medium*		

SPICE AND HERB BREADS

Unless otherwise stated, the following recipes use dried herbs. If you are using fresh chopped herbs, triple the amount given. Any of the herb breads make great egg stratas for breakfast or brunch; leftovers can be used for croutons, or use the dried bread as a basis for bread crackers. Make the medium size recipe on the dough cycle for appetizer pockets, or *Bread Bowls,* see page 26.

OREGANO BREAD

This is an absolute must with spaghetti or lasagna — an often requested bread. Once you have this you'll never go back to plain old garlic bread! Several bread testers have "placed orders" for this when entertaining with Italian meals.

	Small	Medium	Large
water	3/4 cup	1 1/8 cups	1 1/2 cups
olive oil	2 tbs.	1/4 cup	1/3 cup
Parmesan cheese, grated	3 tbs.	1/4 cup	1/3 cup
sugar, optional	1 tsp.	1 1/2 tsp.	2 tsp.
salt	1/2 tsp.	3/4 tsp.	1 tsp.
dried oregano	2 tsp.	1 tbs.	1 1/2 tbs.
bread flour	2 cups	3 cups	3 1/2 cups
nonfat dry milk	3 tbs.	1/4 cup	1/3 cup
yeast	1 1/2 tsp.	2 tsp.	2 1/2 tsp.
Flour equivalent	*2 cups*	*3 cups*	*3 1/2 cups*
Cycle	*basic; timer*		
Setting	*medium*		

PARSLEY HERB BREAD

This is another good bread to serve with chicken. Not as spicy as the preceding Herb Bread, but it adds a nice flavor to the meal.

	Small	**Medium**	**Large**
water	3/4 cup	1 cup	1 1/4 cups
olive oil	1 tbs.	1 1/2 tbs.	2 tbs.
sugar	1 tsp.	1 1/2 tsp.	2 tsp.
salt	1/2 tsp.	1 tsp.	1 tsp.
dried parsley	1 1/2 tsp.	2 tsp.	1 tbs.
dried chives	1/4 tsp.	1/2 tsp.	1 tsp.
dried tarragon	1/4 tsp.	1/2 tsp.	1 tsp.
bread flour	2 cups	3 cups	3 1/2 cups
yeast	1 tsp.	1 1/2 tsp.	2 tsp.
Flour equivalent	*2 cups*	*3 cups*	*3 1/2 cups*
Cycle	*basic; timer*		
Setting	*medium*		

EASY HERB BREAD

Depending on the meal, use your favorite herb: basil, cilantro, oregano, mint or parsley – or you could use a prepared mix of herbs such as Italian, Greek, etc. This bread makes a great egg strata for breakfast or brunch, leftovers can be used for croutons, or use the dried bread as a basis for bread crackers. Make the medium size recipe on the dough cycle for appetizer pockets, or Bread Bowls, *see page 26**, or* Bread Wreaths, *see page 26**.*

water	3/4 cup	1 1/8 cups	1 1/4 cups
olive oil	1 1/2 tbs.	2 tbs.	3 tbs.
sugar	2 tsp.	1 tbs.	1 1/2 tbs.
salt	1/2 tsp.	3/4 tsp.	1 tsp.
dried herbs	1 tbs.	1 1/2 tbs.	2 tbs.
bread flour	2 cups	3 cups	3 1/2 cups
yeast	1 tsp.	1 1/2 tsp.	2 tsp.
Flour equivalent	*2 cups*	*3 cups*	*3 1/2 cups*
Cycle	*basic; timer*		
Setting	*medium*		

GARLIC PARMESAN BREAD

If you're a garlic bread lover, this is for you. Feel free to increase or decrease the amount of garlic powder to suit your taste. Very aromatic and great, of course, with Italian meals. Make sure the garlic powder is fresh (it gets bitter if it sits on your shelf too long), and use freshly grated Parmesan. If you would rather use fresh garlic instead of garlic powder, use 1, 1½ or 2 cloves, minced.

	Small	Medium	Large
water	⅔ cup	1 cup	1⅛ cups
margarine or butter	2 tbs.	2½ tbs.	3 tbs.
honey	2 tsp.	1 tbs.	1½ tbs.
Parmesan cheese, grated	½ cup	⅔ cup	¾ cup
salt	½ tsp.	¾ tsp.	1 tsp.
garlic powder	1 tsp.	1½ tsp.	2 tsp.
bread flour	2 cups	3 cups	3½ cups
yeast	1 tsp.	1½ tsp.	2 tsp.
Flour equivalent	*2 cups*	*3 cups*	*3½ cups*
Cycle	*sweet, basic; timer*		
Setting	*medium*		

ANADAMA BREAD

A very different tasting bread — the molasses gives it just the right "oomph." Legend has it that a fisherman, tired of his wife's cooking, devised this recipe. As he sat down to eat, he mumbled "Anna, damn her" and from then on this was "Anadama" bread.

	Small	Medium	Large
water	7/8 cup	1 cup	1 1/8 cups
molasses	2 tbs.	1/4 cup	1/3 cup
margarine or butter	1 tbs.	1 tbs.	1 1/2 tbs.
salt	1/2 tsp.	3/4 tsp.	1 tsp.
yellow cornmeal	3 tbs.	1/4 cup	1/3 cup
bread flour	2 cups	3 cups	3 1/2 cups
yeast	1 1/2 tsp.	2 tsp.	2 1/2 tsp.
Flour equivalent	*2+ cups*	*3 1/4 cups*	*3 3/4 cups*
Cycle	*sweet, basic; timer*		
Setting	*medium*		

CHRISTMAS ANISE BREAD

Anise adds nice flavor to this bread but is not overwhelming. If you want a stronger tasting bread, you may safely double the amount of anise and other spices. This makes delicious French toast.

	Small	**Medium**	**Large**
milk	2/3 cup	1 cup	1 1/4 cups
margarine or butter	2 tbs.	2 1/2 tbs.	3 tbs.
sugar	1 tbs.	1 1/2 tbs.	2 tbs.
salt	1/2 tsp.	3/4 tsp.	1 tsp.
anise seeds	1 tsp.	1 1/2 tsp.	2 tsp.
mace	pinch	1/8 tsp.	1/4 tsp.
nutmeg	pinch	1/8 tsp.	1/4 tsp.
grated lemon zest	1/2 tsp.	3/4 tsp.	1 tsp.
grated orange zest	1/2 tsp.	3/4 tsp.	1 tsp.
bread flour	2 cups	3 cups	3 1/2 cups
yeast	1 1/2 tsp.	2 tsp.	2 1/2 tsp.
Flour equivalent	*2 cups*	*3 cups*	*3 1/2 cups*
Cycle	*sweet, basic; timer*		
Setting	*medium*		

CHRISTMAS BREAD

This hearty bread for Christmas or any morning is also wonderful with soup or stew.

	Small	Medium	Large
water	1/2 cup	3/4 cup	1 cup
molasses	2 1/2 tbs.	1/4 cup	1/3 cup
honey	1 1/2 tbs.	2 tbs.	3 tbs.
margarine or butter	1 tbs.	1 1/2 tbs.	2 tbs.
salt	3/4 tsp.	1 tsp.	1 1/2 tsp.
rolled oats	1/4 cup	1/3 cup	1/2 cup
bread flour	2 cups	3 cups	3 1/2 cups
yeast	1 tsp.	1 1/2 tsp.	2 tsp.
Flour equivalent	*2 1/4 cups*	*3 1/3 cups*	*4 cups*
Cycle	*sweet, basic; timer*		
Setting	*medium*		

COFFEE SPICE BREAD

This is similar in taste to a brown bread and a great way to use up that leftover coffee — regular or decaf!

	Small	**Medium**	**Large**
brewed coffee	1/2 cup	3/4 cup	1 cup
vegetable oil	2 tbs.	2 1/2 tbs.	3 tbs.
egg	1	1	1
sugar	2 tbs.	3 tbs.	1/4 cup
salt	3/4 tsp.	1 tsp.	1 tsp.
cinnamon	3/4 tsp.	1 tsp.	1 tsp.
ground cloves	1/8 tsp.	1/4 tsp.	1/2 tsp.
ground allspice	1/8 tsp.	1/4 tsp.	1/2 tsp.
bread flour	2 cups	3 cups	3 1/2 cups
yeast	1 tsp.	1 1/2 tsp.	2 tsp.
Flour equivalent	*2 cups*	*3 cups*	*3 1/2 cups*
Cycle	*basic; timer*		
Setting	*medium*		

DOUGH CYCLE

A bread machine gives the ability to make yeasted rolls, breadsticks, and more with relatively little effort. The machine does the initial kneading (the hardest part) and allows the dough to rise for the first time. When the dough is removed, it can be filled, shaped and allowed to rise a second time prior to baking in a conventional oven. See also *Overnight Dough, page* 25.

BAGUETTES OR ETHNIC BREADS (ITALIAN, FRENCH, CUBAN)

While the recipes are wonderful and so very easy in the bread machine, sometimes you might want to present this bread in its traditional form. Use the 3-cup size recipe and make in the machine using the dough cycle. Upon completion of the dough cycle, remove dough and divide in half. On a lightly floured surface, roll each half into a large rectangle. From the wide end, roll the dough in a jelly-roll fashion. Pinch sides closed and place seam side down on a greased baking sheet or perforated pizza pan. Cover lightly with a cloth towel and let rise for 20 to 30 minutes. Heat the oven to 400°. Just before putting the bread into the hot oven, spray (mister-type spray bottle) or brush the bread with cold water. Bake for about 15 minutes until golden brown and bread sounds hollow when tapped.

BRIOCHE

Makes 16

These make marvelous coffee rolls with a very rich texture. It's worth using butter instead of margarine. Be sure to make plenty, as people will go back for seconds and even thirds! This dough will be somewhat moist, which results in a light end product. Add only enough flour to prevent sticking, either while the machine is kneading or after the dough has been removed. To make Overnight Dough *with hot brioche in the morning,* *see directions on page 25.*

milk	1 cup	salt	1 tsp.
butter	4 tbs.	bread flour	3–3½ cups
eggs	2	yeast	1½ tsp.
sugar	3 tbs.		

Remove dough from machine. Form dough into 12 large balls and 12 small balls. Place large balls of dough into muffin tins; press down in the center of each one to form an indentation into which you place a small ball of dough. Cover and let rise for about 40 minutes. Heat oven to 375°. Brush tops of brioches with a mixture of 1 beaten egg and 1 tbs. sugar. Bake for 15 to 20 minutes, until golden brown.

CROISSANTS

Makes 16

Making croissants is not as difficult as one would think from the length of the directions. If you try this once, you will make them many times because you will see how easy it is. Most of the time involved is actually in the rising and the chilling of the dough. Should you decide to make them in the minimum amount of time allowed, you will need approximately 5½ hours. If you desire hot croissants in the morning, you must start the process about 3 hours before refrigerating the dough overnight; and then you need about 1 hour in the morning.

milk	1⅛ cups
vegetable oil	1 tbs.
sugar	2 tsp.
salt	1 tsp.
all-purpose flour	2½–3 cups
yeast	1½ tsp.

Have ready but do not put in the machine

cold butter	1 cup

Allow dough to sit in the machine past the "stop time" with the lid down, so that the total first-rising time should be at least 2 to 2½ hours.

Cover dough right in the pan, and put it in the refrigerator for a minimum of 20 minutes.

Using a lightly floured plastic cutting board, a baking pan or any other rectangular item onto which you can roll dough and pick the whole thing up for refrigeration, roll dough out into a rectangle roughly 9″ x 12″.

While dough rests just a few seconds, knead butter while holding under cold running water. You should be able to make it into a ball easily. Spread butter over rectangle of dough, using a pastry knife or spatula. Leave about $\frac{1}{4}$- to $\frac{1}{2}$-inch unbuttered around the edges.

Fold dough into thirds, much as you would fold a letter to fit into an envelope. Roll dough into another rectangle, fold it into thirds and repeat again so that dough has been rolled and folded a total of 3 times.

Cover dough loosely with plastic wrap and refrigerate for a minimum of $1\frac{1}{2}$ hours, or overnight if you want croissants in the morning.

Repeat procedure for rolling dough into a rectangle and folding 3 more times. You may need to sprinkle flour on dough and/or rolling pin for ease of rolling. Roll into another rectangle and cut into squares (about 4 to 5 inches, depending on the size of croissant you want). Cut each square in half, forming a triangle. Roll each triangle into a crescent shape and place on a well greased baking sheet. Chill for 20 to 60 minutes. Heat oven to 400°.

Bake croissants for 10 minutes, drop the temperature to 350° and bake for another 10 to 15 minutes, until golden.

ALMOND CROISSANTS

Mix 3 tbs. almond paste with the cold butter. Brush top of ready-to-be-baked croissants with beaten egg white and sprinkle with slivered almonds.

ALMOND BUTTER CRESCENTS

Makes 8

These are extremely simple to make: about half my testers said these were as good as the croissants. To make Overnight Dough *for hot crescents in the morning, see page 25.*

milk	1/2 cup
butter	4 tbs.
almond extract	1 1/2 tsp.
eggs	2
sugar	1/3 cup
salt	1/2 tsp.
all-purpose flour	3–3 1/4 cups
yeast	1 1/2 tsp.

Filling

melted butter	2 tbs.
almond extract	1 tsp.

Glaze

1 egg beaten with 1 tbs. water

On a lightly floured surface, roll dough into a large circle. Brush mixture of melted butter and almond extract over dough. Cut circle into 8 pieces, as you would a pie. Roll each piece from wide end to tip of triangle so that it forms a crescent. Brush each roll with glaze. Place on a cornmeal-covered baking sheet, cover and let rise for about 1 hour. Heat oven to 350°. Bake crescents for 15 to 20 minutes, or until golden.

ALMOND NUT CRESCENTS

Sprinkle about 1/4 cup chopped almonds on top of melted butter-almond extract mixture before you cut circle of dough.

ORANGE PRESERVE CRESCENTS

Replace almond extract in dough with orange extract. Instead of filling, place a tablespoon (plus or minus) of orange preserves on the wide end of the crescent. Roll each crescent so that the preserves are tightly encased. Or, use the almond extract and apricot preserves in the same manner.

BRIE CRESCENTS

With or without the almond extract in the dough and filling, brush butter on crescent. Place a slice of brie cheese on the wide end of the crescent and roll so that the cheese is tightly encased.

CROISSANT LOAF

This loaf has flaky layers similar to croissants. Delicious.

water	1/2 cup
margarine or butter	2 tbs.
vanilla extract	1 tsp.
eggs	2
sugar	1/4 cup
salt	3/4 tsp.
all-purpose flour	3 cups
yeast	2 tsp.
To spread over dough	
butter or margarine	3 tbs.

Roll dough into a 1/2-inch thick rectangle. Cut half the butter or margarine into small pieces and place in the middle third of dough. Fold one third over onto top of butter. Place remaining butter, cut into small pieces, on top of folded-over third and fold remaining third over butter. All butter is now encased in dough. Roll dough into another rectangle and fold into thirds, as you would a letter. Wrap dough loosely in waxed paper and refrigerate for about 20 minutes.

Roll dough into a rectangle and fold into thirds 3 more times. Chill dough in the refrigerator if it seems sticky and difficult to work with. Lightly knead dough, shaping into a ball. Place dough in a greased loaf pan (or 2). Cover and let rise for 50 to 60 minutes or until doubled in bulk. Heat oven to 350°. Bake loaf for 30 to 35 minutes or until golden brown.

CINNAMON ROLLS

Makes 12

These rolls are very good and not overly sweet. About two-thirds of the testers liked them as is; the others wanted them sweeter. If you want a sweeter bun, make a glaze out of milk and powdered sugar to spread over the tops while still warm. Baking these rolls in muffin cups makes them rise beautifully and look uniform. To make Overnight Dough *with hot rolls in the morning, see directions on page 25.*

milk	1 cup	**Filling**	
butter	2 tbs.	sugar	1/4 cup
egg	1	cinnamon	1 1/2 tbs.
sugar	2 tbs.	raisins, optional	1/2 cup
salt	1/2 tsp.	chopped nuts, optional	1/4 cup
all-purpose flour	3–3 1/2 cups	**For brushing**	
yeast	1 1/2 tsp.	melted butter	2 tbs.

Remove dough from machine. Roll dough into a rectangle, brush with melted butter and spread cinnamon mixture over butter. Roll dough as a jellyroll and cut into slices of about 1 1/2 inches thick. Place each slice in a muffin cup, cover and let rise for 35 to 40 minutes. Brush tops lightly with melted butter if desired. Heat oven to 400°. Bake rolls for 20 to 25 minutes.

SWEET ROLLS

Makes 12

These are wonderful topped with jam. A special treat. To make Overnight Dough *with hot rolls in the morning,* *see directions on page 25.* *You can also easily make them into wreaths, which make a great gift idea.*

milk	3/4 cup
margarine or butter	4 tbs.
egg	1
sugar	1/4 cup
salt	1 tsp.
all-purpose flour	3 cups
yeast	2 tsp.

After completion of dough cycle, shape dough into 12 balls and place in muffin cups. Cover and let rise for 45 to 60 minutes. Heat oven to 350°. If desired, brush top of dough with additional melted butter just before baking. Bake rolls for 15 to 20 minutes or until done.

PARKER HOUSE DINNER ROLLS

Makes 12

Now synonymous with American dinner rolls, these were originated by The Parker House restaurant in Boston.

milk	1 cup
margarine or butter	2 tbs.
egg	1
sugar	1 tbs.
salt	$\frac{1}{2}$ tsp.
all-purpose flour	$2\frac{1}{2}$–3 cups
yeast	2 tsp.
For brushing	
melted butter	3–4 tbs.
glaze	1 egg, beaten

After completion of dough cycle, knead dough by hand for about 5 minutes. Roll out and cut with a biscuit cutter (or cup). Brush with melted butter. Fold circles in half and place, fold side down, in buttered muffin tins. Cover and let rise for 35 to 45 minutes. Heat oven to 350°. Brush tops of rolls with glaze and bake for 20 to 25 minutes.

HAMBURGER/HOT DOG ROLLS

Makes 12

These are the best. Make plenty and freeze the extras for the next time, if you have any left, that is! Wonderful as is, but good with variations as well. Not only are these great for burgers and dogs, but for sandwiches too.

water	1 cup
margarine or butter	2 tbs.
sugar	2 tbs.
salt	2 tsp.
bread flour	3–3¼ cups
nonfat dry milk	3 tbs.
yeast	2 tsp.

Remove dough from machine. Punch it down and let it rest for 20 minutes. Form into 12 balls, make bun shapes and flatten. Cover and let rise for 1 hour. Heat oven to 375°. Bake rolls for 15 to 20 minutes or until golden.

VARIATIONS

Add 1½ tbs. of one of the following to the dough: sesame seeds, poppy seeds, chives or minced onion. You may also brush the tops of the buns with a beaten egg and sprinkle on sesame seeds immediately prior to baking.

CHALLAH

Challah is a very light and wonderful tasting bread. The dough is somewhat moist, and you should add only enough flour to prevent sticking, either while the machine is kneading or after the dough has been removed.

water	2/3 cup
eggs	2
vegetable oil	2 tbs.
sugar	2 tbs.
salt	1 tsp.
bread flour	3–3 1/4 cups
yeast	1 1/2 tsp.
glaze	1 egg, beaten
poppy seeds, optional	1–2 tbs.

Remove dough from machine and divide into 3 pieces; roll each piece into a rope about 14 inches long and braid on a greased baking sheet. Cover and let rise for about 45 minutes. Heat oven to 350°. Brush top of dough with egg glaze and sprinkle with poppy seeds, if you wish. Bake for 45 minutes.

LITHUANIAN COFFEE BREAD

Tom and Rasa, friends of Lithuanian descent, said this tasted just like the coffee breads their mothers used to make. To make Overnight Dough *with hot coffee bread in the morning,* *see directions on page 25.*

milk	1/2 cup
margarine or butter	4 tbs.
eggs	2
vanilla extract	1 tsp.
salt	1/2 tsp.
sugar	1/2 cup
grated lemon zest	1 tsp.
bread flour	3–3 1/4 cups
yeast	1 1/2 tsp.

Filling

sugar	1/4 cup
chopped walnuts	1/4 cup
raisins	1/2 cup
glaze	1 egg, beaten

After completion of dough cycle, divide and roll dough into 3 rectangles about 9″ x 12″ each. Spread 1/3 of mixed filling ingredients lengthwise down the middle of each rectangle and fold dough over filling to encase it. Braid rectangles together and place in a lightly greased loaf pan. Let rise for about 30 minutes. Heat oven to 350°. Brush dough with beaten egg. Bake for 30 to 35 minutes until brown.

HOT CROSS BUNS

Makes 12

You needn't wait for Easter to come around to enjoy these — with or without the frosting cross. Absolutely delicious.

milk	3/4 cup
eggs	2
margarine or butter	3 tbs.
sugar	1/4 cup
salt	1/2 tsp.
cinnamon	1 tsp.
all-purpose flour	3–3 1/4 cups
yeast	1 1/2 tsp.

Add at end of kneading

raisins	3/4 cup

Frosting

1 cup confectioners' sugar
1/2 tsp. vanilla extract
1 tbs. milk

About 5 minutes prior to the end of machine kneading, add raisins, or knead them in by hand at the completion of the cycle. After a short kneading, let dough rest for about 10 minutes. Cut dough into 12 pieces, shape each into a ball and place in a greased baking dish. Cover and let rise about 35 minutes or until doubled in bulk. Brush with a mixture of egg yolk and 2 tsp. water. Heat oven to 350°. Bake buns for 20 to 25 minutes.

If desired, after buns are completely cool, mix ingredients together for frosting, and drizzle with frosting in the shape of a cross.

VARIATION: Use dried Craisins or any chopped dried fruit instead of raisins.

ENGLISH MUFFINS

Makes 12–15

This is a soft dough. To have dough ready in the morning, *see the* Overnight Dough *section on page 25.*

Water/milk	1 cup
Butter/margarine	2 tbs.
Egg	1
Sugar	1 tbs.
Salt	$\frac{1}{2}$ tsp.
All purpose flour	3 cups
Rapid or quick yeast	$1\frac{1}{2}$ tsp.

Remove dough from machine upon completion of dough cycle. Press dough by hand into a $\frac{1}{2}$-inch thick rectangle on a cornmeal-covered surface. Turn dough over several times so that both sides are coated with cornmeal to prevent sticking. Cut muffins with a biscuit or cookie cutter or use the top of a glass. Place on a lightly greased baking sheet, cover and let rise for 45 to 60 minutes. Cook on an ungreased griddle or cast-iron skillet over low to medium heat for 5 to 7 minutes on each side until golden brown. Cook muffins fairly close together – leaving only a half-inch or so in between. Split open with a fork and serve warm or toasted.

PITA BREAD

Makes 10

The very hot oven makes these breads puff up during baking. Well worth the few minutes involved to make. Easy to have done in time for lunch sandwiches.

water	1⅓ cups
olive oil	3 tbs.
sugar	1½ tbs.
salt	1 tsp.
bread flour	2 cups
whole wheat flour	1½ cups
yeast	2 tsp.

Upon completion of the dough cycle, divide dough into 10 pieces and roll into balls. Flatten each ball into a disk, rolling each one into a circle of about 6 inches. Place on a baking sheet. Heat oven to 500°. Let dough rise for about 20 minutes and bake for 8 to 10 minutes.

BREADSTICKS

Makes 24–32

Far better than the ones you buy in the store. Bake enough to keep on hand. Each of the different toppings changes the flavor of the sticks — try them all.

water	1⅓ cups
margarine or butter	1 tbs.
sugar	1½ tbs.
salt	1½ tsp.
bread flour	4 cups
yeast	2 tsp.
glaze	1 egg white mixed with 1 tbs. water

Cut dough into small egg-sized pieces and roll them into thin ropes. Cover and let rise 20 minutes. Heat oven to 400°. Brush each one with glaze. Sprinkle with salt or seeds. Bake for 15 minutes or until golden brown. The shorter the baking time, the softer they are; the longer the baking time, the crunchier.

SUGGESTED TOPPINGS

coarse salt, sesame seeds, poppy seeds, anise seeds, dried onion bits

CRUSTY PIZZA DOUGH

This recipe makes two large (15") pizzas or three medium (10") pizzas. For lots of ideas on flavored doughs and toppings, see my "Best Pizza Is Made at Home" book.

water	1 1/3 cups
olive oil	2 tbs.
sugar	1 tbs.
salt	1/2 tsp.
bread flour	4 cups
active dry yeast	1 1/2 tsp.

Remove dough from machine and roll into two or three rectangles or circles, depending on the pan to be used. Place on greased pan. Heat oven to 500°. If you want a thicker crust, cover and let rise about 30 minutes. If you want a thin crust, top immediately with sauce, cheese and other desired toppings (don't forget herbs). Bake for about 10 minutes, until crust is brown and cheese is melted.

SUGGESTED TOPPINGS

Basic pizza sauce, mozzarella, basil and/or oregano, any meat or vegetable topping. Salsa instead of pizza sauce, black beans, corn, mozzarella and pepper jack cheeses. Cocktail sauce instead of pizza sauce, cooked and diced shrimp, mozzarella with or without feta and mint.

FOCACCIA

Focaccia (foh-CAH-chee-ah) breads are relatives to pizza and make a great appetizer, or snacks. For best results, use chopped fresh basil the traditional topping) or other herb (cilantro or mint) in the topping. If using dried herbs, use 1 to 2 teaspoons.

water	1 cup
olive oil	1/4 cup
sugar	1 tbs.
salt	1/2 tsp.
bread flour	3 cups
active dry yeast	1 1/2 tsp.

Topping

2 to 4 tbs. olive oil
2 to 3 cloves garlic, minced
1 to 2 tbs. freshly chopped basil
coarse salt (kosher or sea) to taste
(about 1 tbs.)

Remove dough from machine and roll into a 12″ circle or rectangle, place on a greased pizza or baking sheet. Cover dough and let rise in a warm, draft-free location for about 30 minutes. Heat oven to 400°. Press fingertips into the risen dough to form small indentations. Brush olive oil on top of dough. Press minced garlic into indentations, sprinkle basil/herb of choice and salt on top. Bake focaccia on a pizza stone or the bottom rack of the oven for 20 to 25 minutes until golden.

BAGELS

Makes 12

I was ready to give up on a bagel recipe until my frustration finally led me to a local bagel bakery where they shared some hints with me. Here is the successful result.

water	1 cup	whole wheat flour	1 cup
honey	1½ tbs.	bread flour	2 cups
salt	1 tsp.	yeast	1½ tsp.

Let the machine knead the dough once, and then let dough rise for 20 minutes in machine. Even if your cycle runs longer, remove dough after 20 minutes and turn off the machine. Divide dough into 12 pieces. Roll each piece into a rope and form a circle, pressing ends together. You may find it necessary to wet one end slightly to help seal ends together. Place bagels on a well-greased baking sheet, cover and let rise for 15 to 20 minutes. Heat oven to 450°. Meanwhile, bring about 2 inches of water to a low boil in a nonaluminum pan (I use a cast iron frying pan). Carefully lower 3 or 4 bagels at a time into water, cooking for about 30 seconds on each side. Remove bagels, drain on a towel and sprinkle with topping, if desired. Return to greased baking sheet and bake for 8 minutes.

SUGGESTED TOPPINGS

sesame seeds, poppy seeds, anise seeds, dried onion bits

PRETZELS

Makes 15–24

I bet you can't eat just one! Make these treats any size you like.

water	1 1/3 cups
margarine or butter	2 tbs.
sugar	1 1/2 tbs.
salt	3/4 tsp.
all-purpose flour	4 cups
yeast	2 1/2 tsp.
For boiling:	
water	4 cups
baking soda	1 1/2 tbs.

Cut dough into short strips, roll into ropes and shape into pretzels. Cover and let rise on a greased baking sheet for about 45 minutes. Heat oven to 475°.

In a cast iron or other nonaluminum pan, bring water and baking soda to a simmer. Gently lower (by hand or slotted spoon) pretzels into water and cook about 1 minute, turning once. Do not let water come to a full boil. Remove pretzels and return to greased baking sheet. Sprinkle with coarse salt or kosher salt. Bake for about 12 minutes.

NUTRITIONAL COMPARISONS

	CALORIES	PROTEIN (grams)	CARBOHYDRATES (grams)
Flours and Meals (1/2 cup)			
all-purpose	200	5.5	43.0
amaranth	200	8.0	35.0
barley	200	7.0	43.0
bread	200	7.0	41.5
buckwheat	190	7.0	41.0
cornmeal-blue	210	6.0	41.0
cornmeal-yellow	200	4.0	44.0
gluten-vital	200	30.0	18.0
millet	185	6.0	41.0
oat	200	7.0	43.0
quinoa	200	9.0	35.0
rice	200	4.0	44.0
rye	190	9.0	39.0
soy	250	20.0	18.0

	CALORIES	PROTEIN (grams)	CARBOHYDRATES (grams)
teff	200	7.0	41.0
triticale	190	7.0	41.0
whole wheat	200	8.0	40.0
Milk Products (1 cup fresh, or powder mixed with water equal to 1 cup)			
buttermilk	100	8.0	12.0
buttermilk powder	79	7.5	10.7
nonfat dry milk	80	8.0	12.0
skim milk	85	8.0	12.0
whole milk	150	8.0	11.0
Eggs (1 egg or equivalent)			
whole	80	6.0	1.0
white	15	3.0	tr
yolk	65	3.0	tr
substitute	60	6.0	3.0
egg powder	15	0.0	3.0

PERCENTAGE OF U.S. RECOMMENDED DAILY ALLOWANCES

Flours (1/2 cup)	Calcium	Iron	Thiamine	Riboflavin	Niacin
all-purpose	2	25	45	25	30
amaranth	10	80	*	8	4
barley	2	10	15	2	15
bread	2	25	45	25	30
buckwheat	2	8	20	6	8
gluten-vital	*	12	4	*	8
millet	2	20	30	15	6
oat	2	15	30	2	2
quinoa	6	26	10	10	4
rice	2	6	10	2	15
rye	4	15	25	8	8
soy	10	30	25	10	6
teff	10	25	15	4	4
triticale	2	8	15	4	8
whole wheat	2	10	2	6	15

INDEX